COLLINS

Gardening
with BULBS

A Practical & Inspirational Guide

COLLINS

Gardening with **BULBS**

A Practical & Inspirational Guide

PATRICK TAYLOR

HarperCollins*Publishers*

First published in 1996
Reprinted in 2000 by
HarperCollins*Publishers* Ltd
77–85 Fulham Palace Road, London W6 8JB

Text © 1996 Patrick Taylor

Illustrations copyright © Open Books Publishing Ltd

This book was devised and produced by
Open Books Publishing Ltd, Willow Cottage
Cudworth, near Ilminster TA19 0PS, Somerset, UK

Designer: Andrew Barron,
Andrew Barron and Collis Clements Associates

A CIP catalogue record for this book is available from
the British Library

ISBN: 0-00-710382-4

Printed in China

CONTENTS

ACKNOWLEDGEMENTS

I am very grateful to many garden owners who allowed me to study and photograph bulbs in their gardens. I have received an immense amount of friendly help from one of the best bulb nurseries in Britain – Avon Bulbs, where Chris Ireland-Jones and Alan Street received my frequent invasions with the greatest friendliness and shared their deep knowledge most generously. I am very grateful to them. The Royal Botanic Gardens at Kew and at Edinburgh generously allowed me to photograph and gave me much help. Here I should like to thank Jenny Evans at Kew and Alan Bennell, John Main and Ron McBeath at Edinburgh. I learned much about the use of bulbs from the following gardens whose owners gave me generous help: Apple Court (Diana Grenfell and Roger Grounds), Ashtree Cottage (Wendy Lauderdale), Bosvigo House (Wendy and Michael Perry), Chenies Manor (Mrs MacLeod Matthews), Eastgrove Cottage Garden (Malcolm and Carol Skinner), Great Dixter (Christopher Lloyd), Greencombe (Miss Joan Loraine), Kingsdon (Patricia Marrow), Knightshayes Court (Michael Hickson), The Mead Nursery (Steve and Emma Lewis-Dale), The Monocot Nursery (Mike Salmon) and Wollerton Old Hall (Lesley Jenkins).

Patrick Taylor
Wells, Somerset

INTRODUCTION

❧

Bulbs are the most versatile of garden plants. They will flourish in many different sites and climates, and ornament any season. They are too easily associated with spring – every day of the year may be enlivened by their flowers. Apart from the beauty of flowers many also possess strikingly attractive foliage, whether it is the exquisite marbling of *Cyclamen hederifolium* or the bold architectural leaves of the larger irises. Many are undemanding and will form self-perpetuating colonies, happily co-existing with other garden plants. They exist in every imaginable colour and several are exquisitely scented. In size they range from *Crocus minimus*, scarcely 2in/5cm high, to the stately giant *Cardiocrinum giganteum* up to 12ft/3.6m high. Although some have very specific locations in the wild, with climates of great extremes, they will often prove remarkably accommodating, growing vigorously in the very different artificial environment of the garden.

Although in general I have concentrated on bulbs that will flourish in most gardens and are tough enough to survive the hurly-burly of the border, very occasionally I describe plants that may need special protection. Anyone who has been to a well maintained Alpine house will know the beauties of the diminutive species narcissus, tulips, irises and fritillaries. Many of these have such specific needs in the wild that they demand a controlled environment when transplanted to a foreign climate. Some of them, too, are so small that they can easily be damaged when cultivating

9

the garden. However, some of the smaller bulbs, especially those having special cultivation needs, are marvellous to collect and grow in containers in the smaller garden. The miniature species crocuses, fritillaries, irises and tulips whose delicate charms may be swamped in the mixed border are wonderful plants to grow in this way.

This book describes a wide range of bulbous plants, with information on their cultivation, particular virtues and use in the garden. In the term 'bulbous plant' I include different categories of plant which the botanist defines much more precisely – bulbs, corms, rhizomes and tubers. They all have in common the ability to accumulate food and water to be consumed at an appropriate stage in the plant's life.

A bulb is a form of the base of a plant's leaves which has become swollen to provide a means of storing water and food. This allows it to become dormant with enough reserves to enable it to spring to life when seasonal conditions permit. If you cut across a bulb – an onion, for example – you will see the concentric layers of leaf of which it is composed. The fine, dry outermost layer of leaves protects the bulb from pests and infection. Some bulbs (daffodils, for example) are perennial, producing growth from the same bulb, repeatedly over many years. Others (tulips, for example) are annual, with flowers and foliage arising each year from a new bulb formed the previous year. Tulip bulbs grow at different rates and the size of the flower will be related to the size of the bulb. Bulb nurseries will grade bulbs so that a given batch will produce flowers of identical size.

Corms are underground, fleshy stems, resembling a flattened sphere, which provide enough sustenance for one year's growth only. When a flower has been produced a new corm will form above the old one. In addition baby corms – or cormels – are formed about the base of the old corm and perpetuate the plant. These, however, will take some time to grow into corms of flowering size. In appropriate conditions each

Snowdrops, Lenten hellebores and the decorative foliage of *Arum italicum* ssp. *italicum* 'Marmoratum' make a beautiful winter group

corm may produce many cormlets quickly building up a colony of plants. Colchicums, crocosmias, crocus and gladiolus are examples of corms.

Rhizomes are swollen stems, underground or half-submerged, usually horizontal in shape. They are perennial and spread by forming roots and throwing up flowering shoots from time to time. Many irises, some bamboos and Solomon's seal (*Polygonatum*) are examples of rhizomes.

A tuber is a swollen root or stem which may be either completely submerged or close to the surface of the ground. The potato is a characteristic root tuber forming new growth from the 'eyes' in its surface. Dahlias, some species of corydalis, and cyclamen are tubers.

Bulbs in the Garden
Bulbous plants ornament the garden throughout the year. To give something of the richness of plants available I shall go through the seasons briefly describing the bulbous highlights.

Even in deep winter bulbous plants will produce some of the most strikingly attractive foliage in the garden. December and January are brilliantly decorated by the gleaming marbled leaves of *Arum italicum* ssp. *italicum* 'Marmoratum' and the intricately shaped foliage of *Cyclamen hederifolium* whose surface is beautifully patterned in silver, grey and green. This foliage is not only decorative in its own right but provides a marvellous background for the explosion of spring flowers that is to come. In late January they are joined by snowdrops and aconites (*Eranthis hyemalis*) to form a marvellous winter picture. All these plants enjoy similar shady woodland conditions, the same conditions preferred by many herbaceous plants such as hellebores and pulmonarias which associate beautifully with them. Most gardens have areas of shade which are difficult to plant effectively. In quite small gardens it is perfectly possible to create a woodland corner, with plants such as these. They go so well together, and give an air of natural character, that it is probably best to create a naturalistic area for them rather than include them in the more formal parts of the garden where they can seem ill at ease. In large mixed borders, however, there will be places that may provide precisely the right growing conditions for bulbs. Deciduous shrubs, hydrangeas or magnolias, for example, will be leafless at the flowering time of snowdrops, winter aconites and *Cyclamen coum*. In the summer, when such bulbs are dormant, the dry shade under the shrubs' canopy is exactly what they need.

In March the explosion of daffodils gives never failing pleasure. Yet, however essential, they are difficult plants to fit in with other garden schemes. After their flowering the foliage must be left to wither, an unattractive sight in the border and not always easy to conceal. Some of the species, many of which are deliciously scented, make lovely plants for pots. But the hybrids, several of which are easy to naturalise, are really at their best in the orchard or other informal areas of long grass.

Early in the season bulbs give colour and attractive texture of foliage but it is only later that they begin to fulfill one of their other virtues – to provide structure. As border plants this is one of their most precious qualities. Crown imperials (*Fritillaria imperialis*), with

Snake's head fritillaries and blue and white bluebells flourish in the long grass of this orchard

their dramatically beautiful yellow or red-brown flowers in late March also have bold architectural presence. In my garden I grow them under the small tree *Amelanchier canadensis* which is just coming into leaf when they are in flower. They are underplanted with *Anemone blanda*, *Crocus tommasinianus* and *Cyclamen hederifolium*. In the summer they are followed by *Alstroemeria* Ligtu Hybrids, border phlox and *Tricyrtis formosana* all of which flower well under the light canopy of the amelanchier. Crown imperials are also excellent in a little formal box-edged parterre or as an early-flowering ingredient in the mixed border. Other fritillaries, in particular *F. persica* with its tall spires of almost black plum-coloured flowers and *F. raddeana*, not unlike the Crown Imperial but with creamy flowers, are also bulbs with strong structural presence. Other fritillaries have the chief quality of providing splashes of colour and often intricately shaped flowers. The snake's head fritillary, *F. meleagris*, with purple or white nodding flowers, is at its best in a

Illustration opposite:
Celandines (*Ranunculus
ficaria*) and the spring
squill (*Scilla vernum*)
growing wild in an English
wood

naturalistic setting. Flowering in April it is beautiful in the long grass of an orchard mixed with bluebells (*Hyacinthoides non-scripta*) which flower at the same time.

Overlapping with the fritillaries but continuing later are the erythroniums and trilliums. Many of the species of these two groups of plants relish the same woodland conditions. The foliage of both is among the most decorative of all – the bold marbling of trilliums and the curious watery markings of erythroniums. These exotic plants look wonderfully at home in woodland far from their native habitats. Most prefer rich, moist soil, looking marvellous with a background of moss and ferns. In the wrong conditions they will not merely look wrong but will also prove very difficult to cultivate. In my garden I grow erythroniums in a little bed against a north wall among the foliage of hellebores where, later in the season, hostas and the bold leaves of *Kirengeshoma palmata* take over.

The month of April shows the world of bulbs at its peak. Indeed, at this time of year it would be possible to make a beautiful garden using only bulbous plants. A walk in an English wood in this season shows the possibilities. Wild garlic (*Allium ursinum*) and bluebells (*Hyacinthoides non-scripta*), often growing together, form savoury-scented waves of blue and white under deciduous trees. The celandine, *Ranunculus ficaria,* is perhaps a little too wild for the domestic scale of the garden. On the edge of woodland it is often seen flourishing with the spring squill (*Scilla vernum*) making a sparkling mixture of gleaming gold and purple. In the more manicured parts of the garden the various cultivars of the celandine seem more appropriate, with their exotic flowers or foliage.

The various squills flower over a long period. I always relish the appearance of *Scilla mischtschenkoana*, bursting through the soil in February, its flowers starting to open as soon as they emerge. Both *S. messeniaca* and *S. liliohyacinthus* make

The wood anemone (*A. nemorosa*) with ferns in a woodland garden

marvellous underplanting in March and April. In the same season the brilliant violet-blue of *S. siberica* is lovely scattered in odd corners of the garden. Lastly, in June come the majestic plump drumsticks of *S. peruviana*, the only squill to have bold structural presence.

The anemones also make their contribution in March and April. I encourage blue or white *Anemone blanda* to wander at will in borders. They are not invasive, provide ornamental flowers and foliage, and happily share the ground with many other plants. They particularly flourish under a *Magnolia stellata* in a position which later in the season is taken over by daylilies and the giant *Lilium pardalinum*. But in April the mixed border is scarcely performing and this essential anemone makes an exquisite ornament. Its cousin the wood anemone, *A. nemorosa*, is better in a

The tulip 'Angélique' underplanted with variegated hosta

wild setting – among ferns at the edge of woodland, for example. It has very handsome foliage and will form a burgeoning mound, scattered with its crisp white flowers. There are pretty cultivars of the wood anemone (including the lovely violet-flowered *A. nemorosa* 'Allenii') but to my eye the best of all is 'Large-flowered Form' with its bold gleaming white flowers.

April sees the start of the tulip season. It is hard to imagine any gardener not including tulips in a list of essential garden plants. They are very versatile, available in a huge range of colours and span a wide flowering season – as long as three months. Some gardeners treat them as annuals, buying carefully graded new bulbs each year to produce reliable flowers of a uniform size. This labour-intensive and expensive form of gardening, choosing association plants with care, can produce lovely results. Tulips are admirable plants for containers in which it is possible to give them perfect growing conditions. In the mixed border they

can produce exactly the note of colour needed,
associating well with the fresh new foliage of
herbaceous and woody plants. If you can provide the
right conditions naturalised tulips, in a wild setting,
look magnificent. The dazzling yellow *T. sylvestris* or
the scarlet late-flowering *T. sprengeri* are among the
most beautiful tulips that have been successfully
naturalised. Once having seen these flowering
profusely in a meadow or at the edge of woodland it is
easy to become rather impatient with fiddly
arrangements in borders.

Irises flower over a long season and many of them,
unlike tulips, also have the precious virtue of boldly
architectural foliage. Some border irises have crisp
fanshaped leaves which give valuable shape to a mixed
border. Irises vary in character from the exquisite early
flowering miniature alpine sorts to those like *I.
pseudacorus* and *I. orientalis* which have magnificent
blade-like foliage of dramatic architectural form. They
vary, too, in their habitats, from moisture loving species
like *I. sanguinea* to those like *I. unguicularis* which are
at home in the driest of positions. This last, producing
its sweetly scented flowers in December, and for weeks
afterwards, must be near the top of every gardener's list
of essential plants.

Overlapping with the early tulip season are the
camassias. They are not difficult plants but are
surprisingly underused in gardens. They are all good in
the border and one, *C. quamash*, is excellent for the
rough grass of meadows or orchards. The double
creamy-white *C. leichtlinii* 'Semiplena', flowering in
May, is among the most beautiful plants in its season.
Other members of the Liliaceae family also make their
mark in May or June. The rather tender *Asphodelus
aestivus* is worth taking a lot of trouble for. It sends
forth in June bold branching spires of white flowers – a
superlative, shapely border plant which associates
effortlessly with almost anything else. The anthericums
and paradiseas are other liliaceous plants which also
produce strikingly shaped decorative white spires of

flowers in this season.

In June, when many gardens are thought to be at their peak, and a vast range of non-bulbous plants has come into full flower, bulbs still have a contribution to make. Some of these are as bold in structural emphasis as they are in colour. The foxtail lilies (*Eremurus* species) throw out soaring spires of flowers, rising as high as 8ft/2.5m to make marvellous aerial ornaments. The African pokers – *Kniphofia* species – also make a valuable dual contribution of colour and form. Some of these will flower over a very long period, starting in May and continuing throughout the summer. Some are very tall but even the small ones have well-defined presence in a busy border. Very late in the season, in August and September, the larger kniphofias are among the most magnificent border plants. Fashionable garden taste rather turned against them in recent years but sense has prevailed and their brilliant qualities are properly appreciated once again.

Lilies are a particularly precious group of plants, strikingly at home in very different contexts. Some, like *Lilium martagon*, are best in a wild setting: it is one of the best lilies for naturalising in dappled woodland shade. Others, even other species like the magnificent *L. pardalinum*, are superb border plants. Lilies are excellent for the richly planted scheme where their bold and brilliant flowers make an emphatic statement in the profusion of foliage and colour. *L. regale* will harmonise with many arrangements and possesses one of the finest scents of any flower. Lilies, too, perform very well in pots and some of the tender, sweetly scented ones (such as *L. longiflorum*) will ornament a sunny terrace to wonderful effect. Lastly, despite their reputation for naturalising only with difficulty, the species are remarkably easy to propagate from seed, producing flowering bulbs quite quickly.

Crocosmias, formerly known as montbretias, are also plants of high summer which continue to make a contribution over a long period. New cultivars are constantly appearing and some, like the magnificent

A spectacular late-summer border at Great Dixter with blood-red dahlias, the bold leaves of cannas and purple *Verbena bonariensis*

'Lucifer', are plants of tremendous character. They all, of whatever size, have valuable sword-shaped foliage which can give valuable structural emphasis as the mixed border becomes rather formless in late summer. Nor are they all orange and scarlet; some of the yellow forms, such as the late-flowering 'Golden Fleece', are beautiful.

Some of the plants which I describe later in the book are too tender for all but the mildest gardens. But in less favoured climates they make marvellous plants for pots which gives them the additional attraction of providing mobile ornaments. The fabulous African *Albuca nelsonii*, with statuesque foliage and vanilla-scented white flowers, is magnificent in a pot. The eucomis tribe, also from Africa, has similar virtues but, alas, most species smell horrible. But they are beautiful and they may be bedded out in the border very satisfactorily. Some of the more tender gladiolus – like the sweetly scented *Gladiolus callianthus* – may be planted in quantity in a large pot where it will form a sheaf of exquisite white flowers. If well looked after, the corms will multiply with surprising ease. The mysterious almost black *Cosmos atrosanguineus*, with chocolate scented flowers, will in most gardens flourish far more vigorously in a pot than planted out. All these will be flowering in high summer to make wonderful ornaments for the terrace.

Late summer is almost as rich in bulbous plants as early spring. Although some of these (such as the stately galtonias) are of subdued colouring many more explode in dramatic reds, purples and yellows. Garden taste is once more turning to these exciting arrangements to which bulbous plants make such a contribution. Dahlias of the deepest red (such as *D.* 'Arabian Night'), the giant foliage and flamboyant flowers of cannas, and the sharp raspberry red of the little *Alstroemeria psittacina* are dazzling ingredients in the 'hot' border.

With autumn the bulbous season is by no means finished. The garden now sparkles with enchanting nerines, *Cyclamen hederifolium* scattered like jewels in unlikely places, colchicums and sternbergias producing exquisite flowers among the first fallen leaves, and flamboyant amaryllis throwing out their candy pink flowers. As the first frosts clear away tender growth, the exquisite foliage of cyclamens is revealed and in December the indomitable flowers of *Iris unguicularis* appear to remind us that the great bulbous cycle is about to start again.

This brisk tour through the year has only touched upon the major groups and a few others. But there are many more which I have not mentioned, and these are described in detail in the directory of plants in the following pages. Hardiness zone ratings are given for each plant and maps on pages 248–249 show which geographical areas fall into which zones. The hardiness rating, however, is only a broad indication and gardeners should be encouraged to experiment in their own garden. Until you have tried it yourself you can never be certain how a plant will respond.

Albuca

There are about 30 species of albuca, all bulbs, in the family Hyacinthaceae/Liliaceae, most of which are native to South Africa.

Albuca nelsonii
Origin: South Africa
Z: 10

❧ This lovely plant is probably too tender for any but the most privileged garden. However, I have heard of gardeners getting away with it in a well-drained sunny position in Zone 9 with a deep winter mulch. In less favoured gardens it makes a superlative pot plant for the cool greenhouse where it will survive occasional temperatures as low as −5°. It produces a striking plume of glistening green leaves which curve outwards from the centre. A fleshy flowering stem, up to 36in/90cm tall, erupts from the middle bearing a raceme of flowers. The buds are striped with green and the flowers are a waxy white when they open, giving off an exotic scent of vanilla and liquorice. In growth it should be lavishly fed and kept dry when it becomes dormant in late summer or early autumn. On a terrace, especially near a sunny sitting place where its delicious scent may be savoured, there are few more exquisite bulbous plants. Its statuesque shape makes it especially suitable to plant in pots to flank an entrance. In hot weather in the full sun they will need to be watered at least daily if they are in terra-cotta pots.

Allium

The onion tribe is a vast one – with at least 700 species of bulbs and rhizomes in the family Alliaceae/Liliaceae very widely distributed but found only in the Northern Hemisphere. Apart from producing some of the essential culinary flavourings such as the true onion (*A. cepa*), the leek (*A. ampeloprasum* var. *porrum*) and garlic (*A. sativum*), many are also valuable decorative plants. Some, such as chives (*A. schoenoprasum*), are delicious herbs that also produce ornamental flowers – not showy enough, perhaps, for the flower garden but a welcome bonus in the herb or kitchen garden. Some are far too invasive for all but the wildest garden; the pretty rosy garlic (*A. roseum*) runs amok in my garden – apparently reproducing by every means known to botanists.

Allium acuminatum
Origin: N.W. America
Z: 6

❧ For reasons unknown to me this exceptionally pretty onion has never caught on as a fashionable garden plant. Its flowers have dashing character and, in relation to the umbel into which they are gathered, are larger than usual, giving the plant a lively appearance. Opening in June they are a rich deep rosy pink with graceful pointed petals with a deeper stripe down the centre. Up to 20 flowers are gathered in the umbel which, because of the size of the flowers, lacks the crisp drumstick outline of many alliums. The flowering stem rises no more than 12in/30cm, with slender leaves gathered about its base. It does best in rich soil in sun or part-shade. There is a white clone which lacks the charm of the more usual pink form. It may be propagated by seed or by division of bulbs in the autumn.

Allium aflatunense
Origin: Central Asia
Z: 7

❧ The various ornamental onions which form flowers like emphatic drumsticks are immensely valuable garden plants. *A. aflatunense* has handsome glaucous leaves from which erupts a fleshy stem crowned in May

Illustration: *Allium aflatunense* 'Purple Sensation'

by 4in/10cm spheres of purple flowers. The spheres are composed of an immense number of diminutive flowers each held at the tip of a rose-coloured stem. Purple anthers protrude far beyond the tips of the petals. The type is a pretty enough plant but a cultivar with a very off-putting name, *A. aflatunense.* 'Purple Sensation' is a tremendous improvement. Not only is it much taller, up to 36in/90cm, but the flowers are a rich and vivid violet – the sort of colour a rather racy cardinal might wear. It is magnificent in a colour scheme of purples and reds and looks especially beautiful rising from the fresh glaucous foliage of certain hostas (such as *Hosta* 'Krossa Regal'). It will do best in rich, moist soil and will flourish in the semi-shade.

Allium caeruleum
Origin: Asia
Z: 7

❧ This rich blue allium is a native of the steppes. Its stems are slender, rising as high as 24in/60cm, with in June a spherical umbel of flowers, 1 1/2in/4cm in diameter. Each flower is deep blue with an even deeper coloured vein, and blue anthers. By the time it flowers its insignificant grass-like leaves will have withered. It must have a sunny, dry position. It looks very beautiful among smaller shrubs that also have a touch of blue in their colouring such as *Artemisia* 'Powis Castle' or with sea-hollies like the steely blue *Eryngium × zabelii*. It is easily propagated by seed. A form of it, *A. caeruleum* var. *bulbiferum*, also produces bulbils on the flower head.

Allium cernuum
Origin: N. America
Z: 6

❧ This little allium, very widely distributed between Canada and Mexico, has a graceful shape of flower unlike any other. The flowers are arranged in a loose umbel carried at the tip of a stem which curves over at the top. Each flower hangs at the end of a stem which curves upwards and then plunges downwards, so that the flowers resemble little bunches of exotic fruit. The flowers are shaped like rounded lanterns, with white

Illustration opposite:
Allium christophii

stamens protruding. They vary in colour from a rich pink to a deep maroon with hints of magenta. The flowers stems, which are coloured with a plummy bloom, are very slender, allowing the flowers to sway in the slightest breeze. The seed heads are strikingly decorative, with the flower stems stiffening and the seed-pods appearing to shoot outwards like an exploding firework. The flower stems will rise to about 18in/45cm. There is a white cultivar, *A. cernuum* 'Album', not so exciting as the type, and an excellent rich violet one, *A. cernuum* 'Hidcote', which is worth seeking out.

Allium christophii
Origin: Central Asia, Iran, Turkey
Z: 7

❧ This, formerly known as *A. albopilosum*, is one of the most handsomely decorative of the alliums. Its spherical flower-heads, up to 9in/23cm in diameter, are carried on thick fleshy stems up to 24in/60cm tall. The flower buds are lime-green and pointed, opening out gradually in June to form star-shaped flowers with very fine petals. They are violet in colour with a striking metallic sheen, and purple stamens stick straight out from the centre of the flowers. The plumpness of the flower-head is refined by the airy delicacy of the flowers that cover it. The leaves are rather lax, wide, strap-like and glistening. Its colour enables it to mix with many schemes. I have it growing most ornamentally among the brick-red flowers of *Euphorbia griffithii* and it is marvellous among geraniums. After flowering, the seed heads are ornamental. It should have a position in full sun or half shade and it is best in rich soil. It will seed itself gently.

Allium cyathoporum var. *farreri*
Origin: China
Z: 8

❧ Formerly known as *A. farreri* this is among the smaller alliums, rising to no more than 8in/20cm, and is a pretty front-of-the-border plant. The flowers open in June, hanging tassels of sprightly purple flowers each of which has sharply pointed petals giving the flower heads a slightly prickly look. The foliage grows in thick clumps of shining, grass-like leaves. In heavy, wet soil it will seed and multiply, but not invasively. It may be propagated by dividing clumps. It is very decorative in

Illustration: *Allium cyathoporum* var. *farreri*

a sunny position at the front of a border, with pinks and the smaller geraniums. The flower colour is especially attractive against grey. The small artemisia, *A. alba* 'Canescens', which produces a fine froth of silver foliage, makes the perfect background.

Allium flavum
Origin: Asia, Europe
Z: 7

❧ Although this onion forms the drumstick umbel of flowers common to so many other species, the form of the individual flowers is so striking that it is transformed into a plant of very different character. The flowers, which appear in June, are golden yellow, star-shaped, with shapely pointed petals that have an elegant curve. There may be as many as 50 flowers on each umbel which is carried on a stem up to 12in/30cm tall. Each petal has a stripe of green down the centre. Some authorities claim that it is sweetly scented, all I can say is that the clone in my garden has no scent at all. The leaves are decorative, broad, undulating and glaucous green, resembling a tulip's. It will flower best in rich soil in a position in the sun or in part-shade where its glowing colour is seen to best advantage. It seeds itself or clumps may be divided in the autumn.

Allium karataviense
Origin: C. Asia
Z: 8

❧ There is nothing like this immensely decorative allium which is equally striking in foliage and flower. The leaves are very broad, up to 4in/10cm, curving, with a curious metallic sheen, grey flushed with purple.

Illlustration: *Allium flavum*

The spherical umbels of flowers are up to 8in/20cm in diameter, opening in May, composed of countless diminutive stars, a pale violet-grey in colour, becoming paler as they age. The umbels are carried on relatively short stems, no more than 12in/30cm high, giving them the appearance of nestling among the exotic leaves. This is one of the less hardy alliums but so beautiful that it is worth taking trouble to provide the right conditions for it. It must have a sunny position and will not tolerate heavy water-logged soil. It is beautiful growing among other small herbaceous plants, such as geraniums. It looks lovely among the soft glaucous grey leaves and pale violet flowers of *Geranium renardii* which flowers at the same time.

Allium moly
Origin: Europe
Z: 7

❧ This yellow onion has a character all of its own. Its little flowers, opening in June, are grouped in loose umbels but face upwards. Each flower is a resplendent rich yellow star with well separated petals and paler yellow stamens. As the flowers age they become a much paler colour. The plant rises up to 12in/30cm high and the foliage is strikingly handsome, with glaucous grey leaves as broad as 1 1/2in/4cm. In the wild it is found in poor soil in shady places, a position easy to match in most gardens. A shaded site has the additional advantage of preserving the lively yellow of the flowers. It needs sharp drainage. It may be propagated by seed or by dividing the bulbs in autumn. The handsome cultivar *A. moly* 'Jeannine' is a larger plant sometimes producing two generous umbels on a single stem.

Allium nigrum
Origin: Mediterranean
Z: 8

❧ This splendid Mediterranean allium is not often seen but it makes a marvellous garden plant. The flowering stems rise as high as 36in/90cm bearing at their tips stately umbels of flowers shaped either like a broad shuttlecock or a flattened sphere. The flowers, which open in June, are white and their petals curve forward slightly and are marked with a green stripe, and the anthers are a pale yellow, which gives the whole flowerhead a greenish-golden cast. The seeds are

striking – a glistening green or black – appearing as the flowers are still in place. The leaves, grouped together at the base of the flower stems, are very broad, up to 6in/15cm, a glistening fresh green. In the wild this is a plant found in poor soil in waste-land. It needs a sunny position and makes an admirable border plant with its mysterious flower heads rising among other plantings. It will seed itself gently or it may be propagated by dividing the bulbs.

Allium obliquum
Origin: E. Europe, Central Asia
Z: 7

❧ No other allium has quite the colouring of this decorative plant. The flowers in June are spheres, 1 1/2in/4cm in diameter, of pale lime-green flowerlets, like tiny Chinese lanterns, with stamens protruding far beyond the tips of the petals which gives the whole flower head a hairy appearance. The colouring is in appearance like a cold glass of Chablis. The flowering stems, which rise as high as 24in/60cm, are blue-green as is the grass-like foliage. It is best in a sunny position in rich soil and looks very pretty growing among the sprawling foliage of pale creamy-yellow *Scabiosa*

Illustration opposite:
Allium rosenbachianum

ochroleuca or pale violet *Scabiosa columbaria*. This is the kind of small plant of character which, without being showy, makes a decorative contribution to odd corners of the garden. It may be propagated by seed or by division.

Allium rosenbachianum
Origin: Central Asia
Z: 8

This is one of the taller ornamental onions whose flower-head sways elegantly at the tip of a slender stem up to 36in/90cm high. The flowers are gathered together into a spherical umbel up to 4in/10cm in diameter. Opening in May, each flower is a lilac-purple star with a metallic sheen. The rather prominent stamens giving the flower-head a diffused outline. As the flowers fade they are replaced by jade green seed pods which contrast strikingly with newly opened flowers. It makes a wonderful border plant combining great presence with delicacy. It looks beautiful with grey-leafed plants and I have seen it gleaming among the very pale foliage of *Elaeagnus commutata*.

Allium roseum
Origin: Mediterranean
Z: 8

❧ I include the rosy garlic with some misgivings for it has found in our garden, with its heavy, moist soil, the perfect home where it reproduces with prodigal abandon. The leaves appear before the flowers, very thin, like chives. The flowering stems rise 18in/45cm high crowned by a loose umbel of flowers 3in/8cm across which open in May but continue for weeks. They are a fine delicate rose-pink, up to 30 gathered together each at the tip of a wiry stem. As the flowers fade bulbils are produced at the base of each umbel. They become deep red, glistening like something deliciously edible (I do not recommend that you try to eat them). These will be scattered and many new plants produced. The bulb underground also multiplies alarmingly. Although invasive, the foliage is inconspicuous and the flowers, which will intermingle with low-growing plants, are very decorative. In my garden a colony has established itself among very deep purple aquilegias which mix attractively with the pink flowers. It will grow almost anywhere.

Allium schoenoprasum
Origin: Asia, North
America, Europe
Z: 5

❧ The culinary chive is one of the most widely distributed of the allium tribe. Apart from the fact that it is one of the few truly essential herbs it also has great decorative potential, especially in small gardens. The flowers are produced in May or June, small spherical umbels of diminutive flowers of a soft blue-purple held at the tips of very slender, bright green stems which rise up to 9in/23cm. The flowering stems, by the way, are too woody for kitchen use. The finest flavoured shoots are those that first appear, or the secondary growth that will spring up after the first cutting – older growth is coarse in flavour. The decorative value of chives has long been recognised in old-fashioned kitchen gardens where they were often planted in neat rows along the edge of paths. It will grow in shade or in full sun but it should have a rich, moist soil. It is very easy to propagate by seed or by dividing clumps in the autumn. A white form, *A. schoenoprasum* 'Album', also known as 'Corsican White', is particularly pretty and the pink, *A. schoenoprasum roseum* also has its charms.

Allium schubertii
Origin: E. Mediterranean
to C. Asia
Z: 8

❧ This onion is a bizarre but beautiful oddity. The bulb nursery Avon Bulbs describes it as resembling 'a frozen firework in mid burst' and I cannot improve on that. It produces in June a large umbel of flowers, up to 18in/45cm in diameter, among the most imposing of any onion. The individual flowers are star-shaped, a warm pink in colour but their oddity is that they are borne on stems of varying length, some very short but others up to 8in/20cm long. The flower stems are a vivid jade green, making a lively contrast with the pink of the flowers. When the flowers have faded the dead seed-heads are strikingly decorative, with the stiff stems shooting out varying distances from the centre. Flower arrangers go mad about them. It needs a sunny position and will not survive waterlogged soil, needing to dry out completely in dormancy. Plant the bulbs a good 4in/10cm deep and in colder gardens a deep mulch will help to protect them. It is easily propagated by seed which is produced in quantity.

Allium sphaerocephalon
Origin: Europe
Z: 5

❧ The round-headed leek is a European native found in rocky and grassy places, usually in limestone country. It is among the later-flowering of the alliums, producing its flowers in July and August. These are spherical umbels of a vivid red-purple verging on crimson. The top of the umbel is slightly pointed giving it somewhat the shape of an onion and is held at the tip of a stem up to 24in/60cm tall. The flower-head is heavy in relation to the stem, causing it to sway freely in a breeze. Bees love the flowers which can often be seen springing up and down as the bees descend or take off. It makes an excellent border plant, in full sun or part-shade and it will grow in almost any soil. It will enliven many schemes, hotter ones of reds and purples as well as cooler arrangements of pinks and blues. Wishy-washy violet flowers are occasionally seen, much duller than the more common rich purple. There is also a white cultivar. It may be propagated by seed or by dividing the bulbs.

Allium triquetrum
Origin: S. Europe
Z: 6

❧ The three-cornered leek derives its name from the sharply triangular section of its stems. It is one of the most beautiful of the more invasive alliums – few plants of such thuggish disposition have such elegant flowers. These appear in April or May, umbels of sprightly white trumpets, with backward-curving petals crisply marked with green stripes. The umbels hang on one

side of the stem only, with as many as fifteen flowers. The foliage is fresh green, forming bold sheaves among which the flowering stems rise. Stems and leaves give off a rich onion scent when bruised. In the wild it is found in moist shady places in woodland or by the banks of streams. In the garden it will flourish in the shade making a marvellous companion for the fresh new foliage of ferns, Asiatic primulas, *Brunnera macrophylla* and other plants enjoying similar conditions. It will spread quite vigorously and seed itself gently.

Allium unifolium
Origin: California, Oregon
Z: 8

❧ Formerly known as *A. murrayanum* this beautiful American north-west coast species is a very decorative garden plant, though not the hardiest of its tribe. It flowers in early June, producing a loosely-formed umbel of rosy pink flowers. The flowers are marked with a deeper stripe down the middle of the petal and as they age they become much paler, producing an attractive mottled effect of different shades of pink. It grows to a height of about 18in/45cm and, despite its name, certainly produces more than one leaf! It needs a sunny, well-drained site. I have seen it well used at the

Illustration opposite:
Allium ursinum

front of a border rising behind clumps of cottage pinks.
It is beautiful growing through the pale silver-grey
foliage of *Artemisia* 'Powis Castle' which enjoys
exactly the same conditions.

Allium ursinum
Origin: Europe, Russia
Z: 5

❧ In cool woods in England, flowering in April at the
same time as bluebells (*Hyacinthoides non-scripta*), the
wild garlic, or rampons, fills the air with the bracing
whiff of garlic. It does not at all resemble true garlic
(*A. sativum*) in growth. Distinguished tufts of gleaming
leaves – broad, ribbed and undulating – form billowing
mounds of foliage. From their centre the flowers
emerge in April, spherical umbels at the tips of fleshy
stems which rise high above the foliage. The umbels are
composed of diminutive star-shaped flowers, white
with a green eye. Wild garlic, like the bluebells so
inevitably associated with it, is a plant of shady
woodland, relishing deep, moist soil. In the wild it is
also found in hedgerows and on shady banks. In the
garden it is emphatically not a plant for the border. In
an area of wild woodland character, flourishing in deep
shade, it has tremendous character to which is added
the rich smell of garlic, one of the most vivid scents of
spring. You do not need to know how to propagate it –
it will do it for you all too obligingly.

Alstroemeria

There are about 50 species of alstroemeria in the family Alstroemeriaceae/Liliaceae. They are all perennials with rhizomes or tubers.

Alstroemeria aurea
Origin: Chile
Z: 7

❦ This is one of the hardier alstroemerias, formerly known as *A. aurantiaca*. It will make a substantial clump, invariably needing support, rising to 3–4ft/90–120cm high. The leaves are glaucous-grey with an attractive undulating form. The flowers in July are a marvellous warm gold, shaped like an irregular trumpet, freckled inside with deep red spots. They continue well into August and make one of the best late-summer herbaceous plants for the border. I have seen it planted with the almost black red dahlia 'Arabian Night' which echoes the red of the alstroemeria's spots. It is equally valuable in cooler schemes of cream and pale yellow. It will flower well in sun or dappled shade but must have good drainage. It may be propagated by dividing the tubers. The cultivar *A. aurea* 'Dover Orange' is a larger plant with rich orange flowers.

Alstroemeria haemantha
Origin: Chile
Z: 9

❦ This rather tender alstroemeria is rare, but worth seeking out for it has flowers of the most beautiful colour. They open in June, loose trumpets in groups held at the tips of wiry stems. They are a vibrant red-orange in colour and have a presence out of proportion to their size. Flowering stems rise up to 24in/60cm and the foliage is an attractive glaucous grey. It must have a sunny site and requires humus-rich soil. In the garden it would make a superlative contribution to an arrangement of reds, oranges and yellows. I have seen it looking magnificent against the silver new foliage of *Artemisia* 'Powis Castle.' It may be propagated by dividing the tubers in autumn or by seed which may be much easier to find than the plant itself.

Alstroemeria Ligtu Hybrids
Origin: garden
Z: 8

❧ The origins of this garden plant are lost in the mists of hybridisation. It has splendid glaucous leaves, long, narrow and twisting. The fleshy stems, which rise as high as 5ft/1.5m with suitable support, bear lavish sprays of flowers in June. These are irregularly trumpet-shaped and vary in colour from creamy white, yellow to blushful pink. All have a single petal that is marked with bold stripes of a contrasting colour. The result can seem like an explosion in a candy factory but in the right setting the plant has lavish charm, with an air of insouciant abundance. Its habit of growth is lax and it really needs support which in a mixed border could be provided by adjacent woody plants through which it will weave decoratively. It will grow in sun or part shade and needs a rich, moist soil. In full sun some of the colouring will be lost. It may be propagated by division in the autumn.

Alstroemeria psittacina
Origin: Brazil
Z: 8

❧ Previously known as *A. pulchella* this is one of the most garden-worthy of the alstroemerias. Its fleshy tubers stir into life in May, thrusting out pale green leaves followed by stiff, almost woody flowering stems, up to 24in/60cm tall, bearing leaves at regular intervals. The flowers, which open in July, are of splendid distinction. They hang sideways, pointing slightly upwards, long and loosely trumpet shaped (actually more resembling a clumsily furled umbrella). They are a fresh raspberry red in colour, up to 3in/8cm long, and the petals are tipped with pistachio green. The petals are speckled within and without and the anthers are the palest green. Few bulbous plants provide such a beautiful display in late summer, continuing in flower well into August. I have seen it brilliantly used *en masse* in a 'hot' border with crocosmias, dahlias, orange daylilies and flaming red floribunda roses. But it will make an admirable front-of-the-border plant in many schemes. It needs a sunny position in well-drained soil. Slugs are a problem which may be solved by incorporating grit into the planting soil. In colder gardens a deep mulch will protect it in hard winters. It may be propagated by dividing the clumps of tubers in autumn or spring.

× **Amarcrinum**

× *Amarcrinum
memoria-corsii*
Origin: Garden
Z: 8

This is a cross between the two genera, Amaryllis and Crinum, in the family Amaryllidaceae/ Liliaceae. The same cross has also been called × *Crinodonna*. There are two species.

❧ This spectacular late-flowering bulb has great character. It flowers in August producing bold upward-pointing umbels composed of many trumpet-shaped flowers. The flowers are a lively shell-pink with petals that twist slightly and they give off a sweet scent. The flower stems are thick and fleshy, rising to a height of 30in/75cm, erupting from a sheaf of slender leaves. With its flowers pointing towards the sky, there is something triumphant about this plant. It needs the sunniest place in the garden, with protection from a wall. It will do well in quite poor soil but it absolutely demands sharp drainage. It will flower for several weeks and make one of the most striking ornamental plants in the last weeks of summer and the first of autumn. It makes a magnificent plant for a large pot.

Amaryllis

There is a single species of amaryllis, in the family Amaryllidaceae/Liliaceae. The name is often misused for the forced cultivars of *Hippeastrum* often seen for sale in shops at Christmas time.

Amaryllis bella-donna
Origin: South Africa
Z: 8

❧ This splendidly glamorous bulb is a marvellous ornament in the autumn garden. It throws out fleshy, purple-tinged stems which rise up to 36in/90cm and the flowers appear in September or October. They are carried in groups of up to six handsome trumpets of a rosy-pink verging on purple, each 4in/10cm long. The petals are pointed and curve back to reveal a pale throat and long stamens. The flowers are marvellously scented and last for weeks, often remaining well into November. The strap-like leaves appear after the flowers and remains throughout the winter. They should not be removed until the following summer when they are completely browned. It must have the sunniest site you can find and in severe winters it is helpful to protect the foliage with a loose covering of bracken or something similar. The bulbs should be planted quite shallow, with the necks just level with the surface of the ground. In congested groups the bulbs are often forced slightly above ground which, as with crinums, seems to encourage flowering. It lends itself very well to cultivation in pots. It may be propagated by removing bulb offsets. There are several cultivars: *A. bella-donna* 'Hathor' is very floriferous with peachy-pink flowers; *A. bella-donna* 'Johannesburg' has rich pink flowers.

Anemone

There are 120 species of anemones, in the family Ranunculaceae, all of which are herbaceous perennials and those described below are rhizomatous.

Anemone blanda
Origin: S.E. Europe
Z: 5

 In its native habitat *Anemone blanda* is found in rocky places and scrubland in dry, mountainous regions, up to 6,000ft/2,000m. But it will flourish in very different conditions such as those in my own garden, which has heavy soil and high rainfall. The flowers are single, with up to fifteen petals – blue, white or pinkish-violet – appearing in March, unfolding from tubular flower-heads. They are variable in size – from 3/4–1 1/2in/2–5cm. The leaves are intricately lobed and form a mound above which the flowers rise. *Anemone blanda* will flourish in part shade or under deciduous trees and shrubs. It is also very attractive in short grass – I have seen it in an orchard under apple trees. But do not plant it where animals graze, for it contains a narcotic, anemonin, dangerous to livestock. There are some good cultivars including a handsome white one, *A. blanda* 'White Splendour', with larger flowers than the type. Cultivars should be propagated by division in the spring but the type, in an appropriate position, will seed itself univasively, producing attractive variations in colour. *Anemone appenina*, with clear blue flowers, is similar except that it has slightly hairy foliage.

Anemone × lipsiensis
Origin: Garden
Z: 4

❧ This hybrid between *A. nemorosa* and *A. ranunculoides* produces its flowers in April – single, 1in/2.5cm across, a beautiful pale cream-yellow with lemon-coloured anthers. The flowers are borne well above the leaves which are lobed and slender with a red tinge to their stems. I have seen it planted on the edge of a small woodland garden intermingled with white forms of the common primrose (*Primula vulgaris*), conveying the essence of spring. It is also good in a rock garden, in an elevated position so that its detail may be appreciated. It will come true from seed.

Illustration: *Anemone nemorosa* 'Large-flowered Form'

Anemone nemorosa
Origin: Europe
Z: 5

❧ The European wood anemone is a beautiful flower of hedgerows and woodland usually in limestone country. It has prettily divided leaves and single white flowers appearing in March about 1in/2.5cm across with lemon yellow stamens. Various cultivars provide the most attractive garden plants. A group of clones, known simply as 'Large-flowered Form' has strikingly bigger flowers, up to 2in/5cm in diameter, and makes an especially good plant for a woodland setting. The double-flowered *A. nemorosa* 'Alba Plena' is an ancient garden plant, known since at least the 17th century. It has a central ruff of petals surrounded by single petals. *A. nemorosa* 'Allenii' has single flowers larger than the type, a good lavender-blue. *A. nemorosa* 'Robinsoniana', named after the great gardener and writer William Robinson, has similar flowers, not quite so large, carried on striking red-brown shoots. All these will do best in rich, moisture-retentive soil.

Anemone ranunculoides
Origin: Europe
Z: 4

❧ The yellow wood anemone is found very widely in Europe – from Russia to Spain. It has especially attractive fresh green foliage, with each leaf decoratively lobed, like a slender oak leaf. The flowers in April are an astringent yellow, with rounded petals and a silken texture up to 3/4in/2cm across, with a pale green eye. The flower stems are covered in silver hair and the half-open bud, hanging gracefully downwards, is exquisitely formed. This is a plant of deciduous woodland and in the garden it is easy to find a good place for it. In a suitable position it will form a spreading clump which, with its fresh colouring, will illuminate any part of the garden. It may be propagated by division in the autumn. There is a double-flowered cultivar, *A. ranunculoides* 'Pleniflora'.

Anthericum

There are about 50 species of anthericum, all rhizomes, in the family Asphodelaceae/Liliaceae.

Anthericum liliago
Origin: Mediterranean
Z: 7

❧ The St Bernard's Lily is one of the most attractive spring-flowering bulbs, consorting easily with other plants. It is not unlike a white-flowered asphodel but with a character entirely of its own. The flower heads, in the form of racemes up to 10in/35cm long, resemble elongated heads of wheat. They are held on stems up to 24in/60cm tall. The flowers which open in May are single, white with a dazzling silken texture. The yellow anthers are very prominent, thrust forward at the tips of white stamens. The leaves are grey-green, rather lax, forming a busy mound above which the flowering stems rise high. In the wild it is found in high meadows, woodland or quite dry, stony places. It will flower well in part-shade. It is a beautiful partner for other late spring bulbs, in particular tulips. I have seen it planted with the tulip 'Spring Green' whose flowers are a subtle creamy white flushed with pale green.

Arum

There are about 25 species of arum, all tubers, in the family Araceae.

Arum italicum ssp.
italicum 'Marmoratum'
Origin: Europe
Z: 6

❧ There are very few bulbous plants whose chief beauty is their foliage. This arum is among the most valuable, strikingly decorative yet flourishing in awkward corners, such as dry shade. The leaves appear in autumn and make a marvellous winter ornament. They are roughly arrow-shaped, up to 12in/30cm long and quite narrow, with an undulating surface which is a lustrous dark green intricately marked with a marbling of pale green veins which stop just before the edge of the leaf leaving a crisply delineated margin. The whole plant, at its most vigorous in early spring, makes a shapely mass of leaves rising to 24in/60cm. In late spring the fruiting stem appears among the leaves, a pale green pointed shoot which ripens in late summer to a sceptre, 6in/10cm long, of gleaming orange-red fruit packed together – curious and cheerful but not beautiful. Throughout the winter and spring the foliage provides a richly patterned companion for other

Illustration opposite:
Asphodeline lutea

plantings – snowdrops and *Cyclamen coum* in the late winter, followed by *Helleborus orientalis*, Solomon's Seal and lily-of-the-valley. In my garden it grows in dry shade, under the branches of an old yew tree, with ferns and Solomon's Seal, but it will also do well in part shade. It may be propagated by seed or by dividing the tubers after flowering.

Asphodeline

Asphodels in Greek mythology were connected with the Underworld and Homer describes a field of them that were the abode the dead. It is puzzling that such a cheerful plant could have such associations. There are about 20 species, all rhizomes, in the family Asphodelaceae/Liliaceae native to the Mediterranean area and to Asia Minor.

Asphodeline lutea
Origin: Mediterranean
Z: 7

❧ The yellow asphodel, or king's spear, is among the most exotic bulbous plants of the late spring. Its tall stems rise 36in/90cm and are crowned by a mass of flowers tightly packed into a bottle-brush shape. They are golden yellow with long whiskery yellow stamens. The leaves are very decorative – wiry and twisting, pale and glaucous, they writhe about the feet of the flowering stems. It requires a sunny position and, although it needs moisture at flowering time, it does not like waterlogged soil in the winter. It may be propagated by dividing the rhizomes in autumn – the silvery new rosettes of foliage are very attractive.

Asphodelus

The Greek *asphodelos* became in English 'affodil', and eventually 'daffodil' with which, botanically, it has little connection. There are 12 species of asphodel, all rhizomes, in the family Asphodelaceae/Liliaceae.

Asphodelus aestivus
Origin: N. Africa, Canary
Islands, S. Europe
Z: 8

❧ This spectacular and lovely plant is, for some reason, rarely seen in gardens. Also known as *A. microcarpus*, it has a habit of growth unlike other asphodels. It has a branching growth, with flowering stems emerging alternately along the upper part of the

Illustration:
Asphodelus aestivus

central stem, which rises to a height of about 4ft/1.2m, making the whole plant in flower resemble an exotic plume. The flowers are arranged in upward-pointing racemes, each flower bud white and striped in brown. They open in June, white six-pointed stars with a stripe down the centre of each petal and orange-yellow anthers carried on very thin stamens so that they look like tiny insects hovering at the mouth of the flower. The leaves are rather lax, glaucous-grey, and form a sprawling mound from which the flowering stem erupts. It must have sharp drainage and a sunny position. It is a wonderful border plant, throwing up a delicate veil of flowers, but at the same time having statuesque presence. It would make a marvellous plant to dominate a sunny corner or for repeat planting to give splendid harmony to a large border.

Asphodelus albus
Origin: Europe
Z: 6

❧ The European native asphodel is found in the wild in high places up to 6,000ft/1,800m, often in meadow land. Its tall upright racemes of flowers, up to 36in/90cm high, have a splendidly exotic air. In the garden the flowers will appear in May, the long racemes crowded with white or the palest pink star-shaped flowers with lemon-yellow anthers thrusting far out. They are followed by caramel coloured seed-pods, glistening like a freshly-sucked sweet. The foliage is grass-like, glaucous-grey and of rather lax habit. It needs a sunny position in light, well-drained soil. It may be propagated by dividing rhizomes in the autumn or by seed. The white asphodel has an airy lightness that makes it an admirable ingredient for a white border with such plants as the white variegated honesty *Lunaria annua* 'Alba Variegata', late-flowering tulips such as 'White Triumphator' and off-white *Dicentra* 'Langtrees'.

Bulbocodium

There are two species of bulbocodium, both corms, in the family Colchicaceae/Liliaceae.

Bulbocodium vernum
Origin: Europe, Russia
Z: 4

❧ Flowering in February or March this little corm provides a dazzling splash of colour. The flowers which erupt from the ground, virtually without stems, are, in the best clones, a lively rosy-purple. Other clones have rather wishy-washy mauve or white flowers. The flowers open wide in the sun with the pointed petals well separated. They are now more than 4in/10cm high and the leaves, appearing just after the flowers, rise a little higher. In the wild it is found in alpine meadows and in the garden should have an open, sunny site with good drainage. It is easily propagated by dividing the corms. It looks very beautiful among paler crocuses such as *Crocus tommasinianus*.

Illustration:
Camassia cusickii

Camassia

The word camassia comes from the North American Indian name, quamash, which is still a widely used common name. There are about five species, all bulbs, in the family Hyacinthaceae/Liliaceae native to America. All those described below may be propagated by dividing the bulbs in the autumn. The species may be raised from seed.

Camassia cusickii
Origin: N.W. U.S.A.
Z: 5

❧ The form of the flowers of this camassia distinguishes it from other species. The petals are very narrow, and the flowers are profusely borne in a thick upright raceme as long as 15in/35cm – like the most elegant bottle brush that you ever saw. The flowers open in May, the palest possible blue, set off by crisp lemon yellow anthers. The clouds of pale flowers give the plant a wonderful lightness. It looks beautiful among the glaucous foliage and burgeoning flower heads of *Euphorbia characias* ssp. *wulfenii*. *C. cusickii* 'Zwanenburg' is a cultivar with much larger, deep blue flowers which are rather ponderous, much less distinguished than the type.

Illustration: *Camassia leichtlinii* 'Electra'

Camassia leichtlinii
Origin: W. North America
Z: 3

❧ This is a stately plant whose flowering stems rise as high as 4ft/1.2m. It flowers in early May with long upright racemes of flowers which may be as long as 12in/30cm. The individual star-shaped flowers are violet or blue but the best clones are three particularly beautiful cultivars. *C. leichtlinii*. 'Alba' is one of the best white-flowered bulbous plants. Each flower is up to 2in/5cm across, of a lovely silken texture delicately lined with veins. The dark crescent-shaped anthers stand out prominently. *C. leichtlinii*. 'Electra' was an introduction of the nurseryman Eric Smith and has even larger flowers of an especially good rich lilac. In the border it has all the presence of some much

Illustration opposite:
Camassia leichtlinii
'Semiplena'

later-flowering herbaceous plant such as delphiniums. *C. leichtlinii* 'Semiplena' is a very beautiful double cultivar with beautiful creamy white flowers – a marvellous ingredient for a border with a pale colour scheme. *C. leichtlinii* needs rich feeding and will flower well in a partly shaded site.

Camassia quamash (syn. *Camassia esculenta*)
Origin: W. U.S.A.
Z: 5

❧ This is a variable plant but never less than distinguished. From a mound of shining narrow strap-like leaves the flowering stems emerge in April. The stems are up to 36in/90cm tall surmounted by an upright raceme. The lower buds start to open first, revealing star-like flowers with long stamens with sprightly yellow anthers. Different clones will have flowers that range from deep rich blue, through a paler sky-blue to pristine white. It is a superb border plant, associating admirably with other spring flowering bulbs such as tulips. In the wild it is widely distributed, being found both in damp meadows and quite dry places. In the garden it will do well in semi-shade and would be an excellent late-flowering spring plant for the meadow garden or orchard where it will rise above even quite long grass.

Illustration: *Canna*
'Wyoming'

Canna

There are about 10 species of canna in the family Cannaceae. They are all rhizomatous perennials native to Central and South America. These splendid statuesque plants are usually thought of as tender bedding plants. Some, in fact, are hardy in many gardens in most winters but it only needs one really severe bout of deep frost to kill them. Also, they really demand favourable conditions to attain their full size, so the site you choose must be warm, protected and sunny. They are not in any case for timid gardeners, and are too wild and wonderful for the polite border. But in some exotic, jungle-like arrangement they provide in late summer an excitement in leaf and flower which little else can equal in that season. All have bold, upright foliage and are crowned by plumes of flowers which are small in relation to the whole plant but sometimes of brilliant colouring. The rhizomes should be lifted before the winter and stored in slightly moist compost in some frost-free place. They can then be planted out in late spring when the ground has warmed up. They need plenty of nourishment and water to shoot up to their full decorative size in the short growing season available to them in most gardens. Cannas may be propagated very easily by dividing the rhizomes in the spring.

Most cannas available are cultivars which have arisen from complicated hybridisation. However, some of the species and their close relations still provide some marvellous garden plants. *C. indica* 'Purpurea' may grow as high as 6ft/1.8m and has striking deep red flowers. *C. iridiflora* from Peru, supposedly hardier than many, has delicately formed flowers with narrow petals in pink or rich orange yellow and very handsome foliage. *C. malawiensis* 'Variegata' has leaves that are striated in pale green and gold. The flowering shoots have a pink bloom and the flowers are apricot-orange. Of the fifty or so cultivars available commercially 'Louis Cayeux' is an excellent pale pink and 'Wyoming' is a vibrant orange with bronze-tinged foliage.

Cardiocrinum

Cardiocrinum giganteum
Origin: Himalayas
Z: 7

There are three species of cardiocrinum, in the family Liliaceae/Liliaceae.

❧ There is nothing at all like this giant, aristocratic bulb which takes years to produce its flowers and needs very special conditions. However, it gives unique and spectacular pleasure, well worth waiting for. Its flowers in late June are immense white trumpets, each up to 8in/20cm in length, opening out sharply at the tips revealing a plummy interior. The flowers give off a deep, rich, exotic scent which few garden plants can equal. It needs a shady position in rich, moist soil that is, nonetheless, well drained for in waterlogged places the bulbs, over a long period of time, will rot. In appropriate conditions it will, after six or seven years from sowing, throw out its immense, stiff flowering stem, rising as high as 12ft/3.6m, crowned with as many as 20 downwards sloping flowers. It is monocarpic (i.e. flowering once only), producing huge quantities of seed but mature bulbs will split and may be divided, These new bulbs will produce a flowering stem in about four years. Much nourishment is need to support these fast growing, giant stems and a deep mulch of well-rotted manure in the spring will help. They also require moisture at growing time. The only place for it is in a woodland garden in the large-scale context of trees and shrubs. In a planned border it must have substantial companion planting.

Chionodoxa

The name of these bulbs, of which there are six species, means 'glory of the snow'. They are in the family Hyacinthaceae/Liliaceae and all come from the Mediterranean region.

Chionodoxa luciliae
Origin: Turkey
Z: 4

❧ The blue glory of the snow is one of those miniature plants, in itself without tremendous presence, which can enliven a corner or, planted in quantity, produce a dazzling splash of colour. It grows 6in/15cm high and the flowers in February or March are a sprightly clear blue fading to a chalk-white centre with a pale yellow eye. The flowers are star shaped, with pointed petals, held above fresh green pleated leaves. It will flower well in part shade, the sprightly blue showing to great advantage. In the wild it is found in stony, poor soil in harsh mountain conditions. In the more benign environment of the garden in a temperate climate it will establish itself vigorously. It may be propagated by dividing clumps of bulbs in the autumn or after flowering, or by sowing seed. It makes an excellent underplanting for deciduous shrubs such as magnolias. The first flowers of the early-flowering *Magnolia stellata* will overlap with the last flowers of *Chionodoxa luciliae*. It also associates well with other spring bulbs – with the paler yellow daffodils, for example. The slightly later-flowering *C. forbesii* is similar, with deeper blue flowers; there is a very unsatisfactory blotchy pink cultivar, *C. forbesii* 'Pink Giant', which sounds as horrible as it looks.

Colchicum

There are over 40 species of colchicum, all corms, in the family Colchicaceae/Liliaceae very widely distributed in Asia, Africa and Europe. They are often misleadingly referred to as 'autumn crocuses'.

Colchicum agrippinum
Origin: Garden
Z: 6

❧ This exquisite colchicum provides a dazzling sight in September. The flowers are exquisitely formed – rosy-purple trumpets of long, narrow, pointed petals held triumphantly at the tips of pale stems. The petals are speckled with vague chequered spots and the anthers are a rich purple. It rises no more than 4in/10cm and in the right conditions (not hard to provide) it will form generously floriferous clumps. The narrow, pointed leaves appear well after the flowers. It is unknown in the wild: its origin is uncertain but it is thought to be a hybrid of *C. autumnale* and *C. variegatum*. It is best in a well drained site and it will flower well in dappled shade. I have seen it looking beautiful with the newly opened foliage of *Cyclamen hederifolium*. It is easily propagated by dividing the corms in the spring or by sowing fresh seed.

Colchicum byzantinum
Origin: Garden
Z: 6

❧ This is one of the oldest garden flowers, being known to the great botanist and gardener Carolus Clusius at the beginning of the 17th century. It flowers in September, an admirable pink-purple, with much darker stamens. It is very vigorous and will establish

itself easily bringing the atmosphere of spring
exuberance to the autumn garden. It rises to about
8in/15cm high and its flowers are neatly formed. The
leaves, appearing well after the flowers and taller than
them, are very striking, ribbed and up to 6in/15cm
wide. There is a white cultivar, *C. byzantinum* 'Album'.

Colchicum speciosum
Origin: Caucasus, Iran,
Turkey
Z: 6

≿ The appearance of this large colchicum in autumn is
always an exhilarating surprise. As the rest of the
garden is starting to go to sleep, its leafless flowering
stems shoot through the earth unfurling their purple
flowers in October which rise to 8in/15cm high. Their
leaves, too, are a great surprise for they appear in the
following spring, so large, broad and gleaming that you
find it almost impossible to believe that they are related
to the same plant. The flowers are among the most
cheerful autumn plants, often to be seen thrusting
through the fallen leaves of deciduous shrubs and trees.
The flower is 3in/8cm long and remains neatly cupped,
with the petals opening out only slightly in the
brightest sunshine. It is a tough plant, growing in the
wild in mountain pastures as high as 10,000ft/3,000m.
In the garden it would make a marvellous meadow
plant were it not for the dilemma of when to cut the
grass. It is not difficult as to soil and will naturalise
obligingly. There is a most beautiful white cultivar, *C.
speciosum* 'Album', which flourishes in my heavy clay.

Convallaria

This is one of those unusual genera of which there is
only a single species, in the family
Convallariaceae/Liliaceae.

Convallaria majalis
Origin: Northern
Hemisphere
Z: 3

≿ The lily-of-the-valley has the most delicious scent
of any garden plant, with a piercing freshness which is
irresistible. For that reason alone it is an essential
presence in the garden. It is also very easy to please – it
even grows through the tarmac in my yard. The
emerging shoots look very distinguished, fleshy and
suffused with a grey bloom. The leaves are oval and
crisply pointed, an attractive glaucous green, pleated

down the centre and marked with fine striations. The
flowering stems are 6in/10cm long and the flowers
which appear in May are creamy white, diminutive
bells the tips of whose petals reflex backwards. The
flowers are generously borne, up to a dozen on each
arching stem. In the wild this is a plant of woods and
meadows, found growing as high as 8,000ft/2,400m. In
the garden it will flourish in the shade, relishing a cool
position. I grow it in rather heavy soil, which seems to
please it, among ferns, hellebores and *Brunnera
macrophylla.* I have seen it grown in pots and brought
indoors to flower early and fill a room with its lovely
scent. Flat-dwellers with window boxes may grow it
successfully, with the perfume wafting in through the
open window. There are various cultivars of which
C. majalis 'Fortin's Giant' is simply a larger version of
the type – almost twice its height. The variegated form,
C. majalis variegata, always seems to me a rather feeble
little plant. Lilies-of-the-valley are very easily
propagated by dividing the rhizomes in the autumn.

Corydalis

The name corydalis comes from the Greek for the crested lark which is said to resemble the shape of the flowers. There are about 300 species, in the family Papaveraceae. They are all herbaceous perennials some of which are rhizomes or tubers.

Corydalis flexuosa
Origin: W. China
Z: 7

&❧ Few plants have spread so quickly into gardens as this dazzling newcomer which was introduced into cultivation in the U.S.A. in 1987 and in Europe in 1989. It spreads by rhizomes, forming a vigorous mound of beautiful, fern-like foliage about 6in/15cm high. Each leaf is finely cut, pale green, with a reddish base and spots on the leaf. The flowers appear in April and continue for weeks, producing flowers intermittently throughout the season. They are held handsomely above the foliage, a wonderful rich blue with a hint of green. Four clones show slight but attractive variations: *C. flexuosa* 'Purple Leaf' has striking purple-bronze foliage and a rich violet-blue flower; *C. flexuosa* 'Père David' has paler blue flowers; and the foliage and flower buds of *C. flexuosa* 'China Blue' are flushed with pink. A fourth cultivar, *C. flexuosa* 'Blue Panda',

Illustration: *Corydalis flexuosa* 'Père David'

was collected by the American nurseryman Reuben Hatch who was responsible for first introducing the plant into cultivation in 1987. This has especially vivid blue flowers, with a characteristic upward-pointing curved spur, and bright green finely cut leaves. In the wild *Corydalis flexuosa* is found in humus-rich moist soil in woodland. I grow it close to a high north-facing wall in heavy soil, which seems to suit it. The flowers are produced over a long period – showing an especially intense colouring in cold weather. The foliage remains ornamental throughout the season. It makes a beautiful underplanting to hellebores which enjoy similar conditions. It is easily propagated by dividing the rhizomes in late summer or in autumn.

Corydalis lutea (syn. Pseudofumaria lutea)
Origin: Europe
Z: 6

❧ This European native is the type of easy plant – some say too easy – which inconspicuously adds character and visual texture to the garden. It has very ornamental foliage, an excellent glaucous grey-green, with finely cut and lobed leaves. The little flowers in May are a sharp lemon yellow, shown off strikingly by the foliage. In the wild it is found in rocky limestone country but I find it grows well in my rich, moist soil, ornamenting shady corners. It spreads by rhizomes by which it is easily propagated. There is a white form, *C. lutea* 'Alba', but far better is the white-flowered

Illustration:
Corydalis lutea

C. ochroleuca (also known as *Pseudofumaria alba*), which is fibrous-rooted, with delicate putty-white flowers with spots of green on the lip and lemon throats. The foliage is particularly finely cut and the fleshy shoots flushed with dusty pink. It grows well in the shade and makes an admirable partner for all sorts of other shade-loving perennials. Both will form burgeoning mounds, up to 10in/25cm high. They will seed themselves gently, showing a particular liking for the limestone walls of my garden where they attach themselves, hanging in splendid swags.

Corydalis solida
Origin: Asia, Europe
Z: 6

With its upright racemes of purple flowers in April this tuberous corydalis is a cheerful native plant of hedgerows and woodland found very widely in Europe. It has the decorative finely-cut leaves of most of its tribe. The wild type would scarcely earn its place

Illustration: *Corydalis
solida* 'George Baker'

in the garden, except in a wild corner. But a marvellous
cultivar, *C. solida* 'George Baker', is entirely
garden-worthy. It has flowers of a rich, warm
salmon-pink which are beautifully displayed against
the glaucous foliage. It forms a plant no more than
6in/15cm high and, is an excellent subject for the alpine
garden or rockery. I have seen it looking distinguished
overflowing the rim of a terracotta pot. It must have a
well-drained position.

Cosmos

There are about 25 species of cosmos in the family
Compositae. They include those useful half-hardy
annuals with finely cut leaves which are cultivars of
two Central American species *C. bipinnatus* and *C.
sulphureus.*

Cosmos atrosanguineus
Origin: Mexico
Z: 8

&❧ This tuber produces flowers of an extraordinary
colour – a very deep chocolate-purple, almost black
when they first open. They appear in June or July and
carry on for many weeks, deep into autumn. They are
1 1/2in/4cm across and give off a sweet, vanilla scent
with overtones of chocolate. It has attractive deeply cut
foliage and the finely hairy stems are flushed with
purple. It absolutely needs rich well-drained soil and
plenty of sun. The tuber is relished by slugs, and many
plants have been eaten in the heavy slug-laden soil of

my garden. However, it is a magnificent plant for pots, making a marvellous contribution to an arrangement of red and purple. It is also very easy to propagate, by semi-ripe cuttings in later summer, so in less benign gardens it may be treated as a tender bedding plant.

Illustration:
Crinum × powellii

Crinum

There are well over 100 species of crinum, in the family Amaryllidaceae/Liliaceae, all bulbs and distributed widely in the tropics and the southern hemisphere. Only a handful are available commercially and these tend to be species that are hardy enough to survive in the garden in warmer places.

Crinum bulbispermum
Origin: South Africa
Z: 6

❧ This species crinum is, with *C. moorei,* one of the parents of the hybrid *C. × powellii* described below. It has a strong character all of its own and is well worth seeking out. The flowering stems rise to 4ft/1.2m and the flowers open in late July or August. These are pale pink trumpets, smudged on the backs of the petals with rosy purple, and giving off a delicious sweet scent. The flowers are most elegantly held, curving slightly downwards on long arched stems. The strap-like leaves are a decorative glaucous green. It must have a sunny position and rich soil. Like *C.* × *powellii* it seems to flower best when the bulbs are fairly constricted. It makes a magnificent bulb for a substantial pot.

Crinum × *powellii*
Origin: Garden
Z: 6

❧ Few bulbous plants have such presence in the garden. Masses of leaves are produced, broad and glistening, from which the thick flower stems, rising 36in/90cm, emerge to produce their flowers in August. These are wonderfully elegant, with the buds curving out from upright flower heads, resembling the beak of an exotic bird before they open. The flowers are the palest pink, gently trumpet-shaped, with the petals curving crisply backwards at the tip. The petals have the texture of silk and the stamens with their curving anthers crowd the throat. The flowers give off a sweet scent and last for many weeks making one of the most exciting plants that performs late in the season – I have seen them still in flower in October. To flower well it needs a sunny position. The books say that it needs sharp drainage but I have grown it successfully in heavy clay. The bulbs should not be planted too deeply – their necks should just break the surface. It is said to flower best when the bulbs are packed together or restricted within the confines of a pot. The white cultivar *C.* × *powellii* 'Album' is, if anything, even more beautiful than the type.

Crocosmia

There are about six species of crocosmia in the family Iridaceae all native to South Africa. They were formerly known as montbretia. They interbreed with great ease so that the true identity of both species and cultivars is difficult to establish. However, they are essential garden plants, easy when established and ornamental both in foliage and in flower. The flower

Illustration: *Crocosmia* 'Golden Fleece'

juts sideways, a spike of flowerlets whose petals curve backwards, in many cases thrusting the stamens far out. They will flower well in part shade or full sun and are at their best in moisture-retentive soil, needing water as the flowers develop. In British gardens it is striking how well they do in the wet west of England or on the west coasts of Ireland and Scotland. Most are hardy to Zone 7 but in many colder places if the corms are planted deep and perhaps mulched in the winter they will have a good chance of surviving. The species, such as *C. masoniorum* and hybrids like *C.* × *crocosmiiflora* are pretty enough but the most valuable garden plants are certainly to be found among the various cultivars. *C.* 'Lucifer' is a magnificent July-flowering variety with vibrant scarlet flowers and particularly handsome foliage, dark green, quite broad and upright. *C.* 'Rowallane' is similar in stature, also flowering in July, with very large pale apricot flowers. *C.* 'Emily Mackenzie' is much later flowering, in August and September, with excellent rusty-orange flowers splashed with darker spots within the flowers. It grows

Illustration:
Crocosmia 'Lucifer'

to about 24in/60cm tall, delicately formed. *C.* 'Golden Fleece' (formerly *C.* 'Citronella') is another of the smaller kinds but with beautiful pale yellow flowers, appearing late in the summer and often continuing into the autumn – as late as October in my garden. C. 'Solfatare' is another yellow-flowered variety that flowers in late summer and autumn. *C.* 'Red Knight' will grow as tall as 36in/90cm, with marvellous deep red flowers in August or September.

Crocosmias make a contribution to the late summer border which few other plants equal. Even before their flowering period the stiff, blade-like leaves are an attractively firm shape in a densely planted border. In flower, with their shades of yellow, apricot or red, they give fresh colour when other herbaceous plants are flagging. The reds and oranges are superlative as ingredients in a hot-toned border. They are magnificent with alstroemerias, dahlias, daylilies and appropriate bedding plants, perhaps set against a background of the deepest purple foliage of *Cotinus coggygria.* The yellow-flowered kinds look good with orange-flowered plants such as *Lilium pardalinum* or *Alstroemeria aurea* or with the blues of delphiniums. Crocosmias are easy to propagate by dividing the corms which can become very congested.

Crocus

There are about 80 species of crocus, all corms, in the family Iridaceae native to mid Europe, the Mediterranean region and Central Asia – in a very wide range of habitats from the banks of the Mediterranean to the mountainous regions of Afghanistan. For the garden the most precious species are those that will establish trouble-free colonies. Some, too delicate and too demanding in terms of site for life in the border, are only appropriate for the Alpine house or trough.

Crocus gargaricus
Origin: Turkey
Z: 7

This is not the toughest of crocuses but it is so beautiful that it is worth any trouble taken in its cultivation. It flowers in March, ghostly shoots, the palest creamy white, thrusting from the soil from which the rounded flower heads emerge. These are the loveliest warm golden yellow, finely veined in a darker shade. In full sun they open out, showing their pointed petals. In the wild *C. gargaricus* grows in meadows, up to 10,000ft/3,000m. In the garden it should be given a well-drained site, in the sunniest place you can find. In a cold-frame or unheated greenhouse it is easy to provide the perfect conditions, bringing the pot into the house when flowering is about to start, to provide one of the most beautiful house-plants imaginable.

Crocus goulimyi
Origin: Greece
Z: 7

❧ This is one of the most beautiful of the autumn-flowering crocuses. Its flowers, which appear in September or October, are sweetly scented and vary from pale to richer lilac, borne on pale stems which rise 6in/10cm high. The petals are marked with finely etched lines in deeper purple and the anthers are egg-yolk yellow. In the wild it is found in rocky places in limestone country. In the garden it should be given a sunny site and appears to flourish in all but the most waterlogged soil. It may be propagated both by seed and by division of corms. There is a beautiful white cultivar *C. goulimyi* 'Mani White' (syn. *C. goulimyi* 'Albus').

Crocus minimus
Origin: Mediterranean
Z: 8

❧ This enchanting little crocus is not a plant to make much of an impact in the garden. But it is very beautiful and it is well worth trying to find a position that will provide the conditions it needs. Its flowers, which appear in February or March, are a rich lilac colour, opening quite flat in the sun, and with rounded petals. The petals are marked with a deeper purple feathering, most striking on the back, and the stamens are deep golden yellow. The flower stems rise no more than 2in/5cm and the narrow grass-like leaves are much taller, half concealing the flowers. In the wild it is found in sandy soil sometimes, in Corsica or Sardinia, at the edge of a beach. It is a plant for the rock garden or for a pot or trough raised up on a sunny terrace where its exquisite flowers may be admired close-up.

Crocus sieberi
Origin: Greece
Z: 7

❧ This is not the hardiest crocus but it is one of the prettiest. The flowers in February or March are pale lilac – there is a distinguished deeper purple form *C. sieberi* var. *atticus.* All have a striking orange-yellow throat to the flower and narrow grass-like foliage. In its native habitat *C. sieberi* is found in the mountainous regions of Greece, exceedingly dry in the summer. In cooler countries it must have a sunny position and good drainage. I grow it at the foot of the common rosemary (*Rosmarinus officinalis*) in a south-facing border. Other small shrubs of a Mediterranean character – artemisias, lavender and sages – will provide good companion plants which also enjoy the same conditions. *C. sieberi* 'Bowles White' is a beautiful pure white cultivar.

Crocus tommasinianus
Origin: E. Europe
Z: 5

❧ In early February the pale mauve flowers of *Crocus tommasinianus* are an exhilarating sight. Up to 4in/10cm high, they are the palest grey-mauve on the outside, a deeper violet within, with striking yellow

stamens which give off a powerful smell of saffron in the sun. The leaves are very narrow, almost like grass, marked with a pale stripe that emphasises their elegance. All gardeners should try and provide a site for this marvellous crocus that will allow it to multiply and thrive. In its natural habitat it is a woodland plant and in the garden should have at least semi-shade. I have it growing under a small ornamental deciduous tree, *Amelanchier canadensis,* which seems to give it the conditions it needs, providing summer dormancy in dry soil in the shade of the tree. It seeds itself lavishly, even spreading into the adjoining lawn. I have seen it flourishing in informal areas of grass which should have been cut as late as possible to allow the crocus to be visible. It associates well with other spring-flowering plants such as snowdrops, aconites and *Anemone blanda.* There are some good forms, including a lovely pure white one, *C. tommasinianus albus.* There are several cultivars which add nothing to the quality of the type.

Crocus vernus
Origin: E. and S. Europe
Z: 4

᭞ The species has a slightly cupped, rounded flower, mauve or white, up to 4in/10cm high. It flowers in February or March and is very rarely seen in its wild type, for it is the origin of countless cultivars which provide plants for large-scale planting in public gardens. Individually many of these cultivars are rather coarse but *en masse,* especially with carefully chosen combinations of colour, they can be very effective. In short grass, under deciduous trees, they will make a dazzling spring spectacle.

Cyclamen

There are about 20 species of cyclamen, all tubers, in the family Primulaceae. The word comes from the Greek *kyklos,* a spiral, referring to the twisting stem of the seed pod. They come from Europe and the Mediterranean area, with one species from central Africa. The tubers may be bought when dormant or when in leaf. Different species produce their roots from different surfaces of the tuber so, if planting when dormant, it is best to plant it on its side – it will settle into the correct position of its own accord. Always buy a generous quantity and plant them in a substantial group – one or two merely look absurd. In appropriate conditions all the cyclamen described below will self seed easily. In some years this will be so prolific that it is best to transplant seedlings to less crowded areas. Despite their delicate appearance they are very tough plants and among the most versatile. Different species will flower in winter, spring and late summer and in each case their foliage continues to provide ornament long after the flowers have gone.

Cyclamen coum
Origin: Caucasus
Z: 6

᭞ The winter-flowering cyclamen provides a splash of brilliant colour given by no other hardy plant in that season. The flowers in January are a cheerful purple-pink, raised well above the foliage. Before they open, the buds curve downwards elegantly from their red-brown stems. In a community of plants the white form frequently appears creating a striking effect like some summer fruit splashed with cream. The leaves are

Illustration opposite:
Cyclamen coum

rounded and of a leathery texture with handsome markings: at the centre of each leaf there is a darker shape of an ivy-leaf edged with a vague silver outline. In young plants the underside of the leaf – which you will never see unless you turn it over – is a rich maroon. It will flourish in shade or part-shade but I have seen it well established in the short grass of a sunny orchard. It flowers in the same season as other small bulbous plants such as snowdrops and winter aconites (*Eranthis hyemalis*) which together make a brilliant winter picture. There are several selected forms, those with especially pale, silver colouring to the foliage being especially appreciated. *C. coum* 'Maurice Dryden' is a beautiful one with white flowers. There is a particularly attractive form with a clear pink flower, *C. coum roseum*.

Cyclamen hederifolium (syn. C. neapolitanum)
Origin: S. Europe, Turkey
Z: 6

❧ The so called ivy-leafed cyclamen produces leaves that roughly resemble those of ivy but they are very variable and, in their marking, far more intricate and beautiful than any ivy. The flowers appear in late summer just at the moment when most other perennial plants seems to have produced their last flowers. The flowers are diminutive – no more than 3/4in/2cm long – like little sails, held aloft on brown-tinged stems.

They vary in colour from a cheerful purple pink – sometimes attractively astringent – to pure white. In late autumn the spherical seed-heads are held at the tips of intricately coiled stems. Before the flowers have faded the leaves start to unfurl revealing the most decorative aspect of this cyclamen. The leaves are bold, up to 4in/10cm long, and varied in shape – some pointed, some almost circular and others heart-shaped or finely scalloped. They have deep veins and are dappled with marbling. Their colour varies from deep green to a much lighter colour of pale silver green. In a vigorous clump the leaves will crowd together and overlap making a striking pattern. They remain throughout the winter, forming a wonderful background to winter-flowering plants such as snowdrops, cyclamen and aconites. They continue into the summer, falling only in June. In the wild it is found in shady places, in woodland or in olive-groves. In the garden it will do well in a north-facing position or scattered round the trunk of a deciduous tree or shrub.

Cyclamen purpurascens
Origin: Europe
Z: 6

❧ This cyclamen produces its flowers in late summer and early autumn. They are a lively carmine pink with a much darker patch at the base of the flower. The flowers are deliciously scented and a substantial colony will suffuse the air with its perfume. The leaves are rounded or gently heart-shaped, up to 3in/8cm across, with purple markings on the underside and decorative marbling on top, often with a pale margin surrounding an ivy-leaf shape at the centre. In the wild it is found in rich calcareous soil and in the garden is best in moist soil in dappled shade. It is beautiful among ferns and hellebores at the edge of a shady woodland garden.

Cyclamen repandum
Origin: Mediterranean
Z: 7

❧ This is the spring-flowering counterpart of *C. hederifolium* with distinctive virtues of its own. Its flowers appear in April, a sprightly pink-magenta, with twisted petals resembling a rather muddled ship's propeller, and marked with a splash of purple at the base. The flowers are deliciously scented – the perfume very striking on warm spring day. The flowers are held

well above the foliage on red-brown stems and the
flowering shoots will scramble through low-growing
plants scattering brilliant dabs of colour. The leaves,
appearing at the same time as the flowers, are scalloped,
finely toothed, loosely heart-shaped and delicately
marbled with paler green. At the centre of each leaf
there is the darker shape of an ivy-leaf. They are just as
beautiful as those of *C. hederifolium* but do not have
the same decorative impact, being soon overwhelmed
by the rush of summer plants. In the wild it is a
woodland plant, often found in quite dry places in pine
forests. In the garden it is very versatile but always at
its best with some shade. The flowers appear at a time
when yellow, blue or violet are the dominating colours.
It looks beautiful among ferns or with snake's head
fritillaries (*Fritillaria meleagris*), erythroniums, wood
anemones (*Anemone nemorosa*) and the pale violet
Scilla messeniaca all of which flower at the same time. I
have also seen it intermingled with inky-purple grape
hyacinths (*Muscari armeniacum*), like a spread of rare
mixed jewels. It may be grown successfully in a
meadow garden. A subspecies, *C. repandum* ssp.
peloponnesiacum, has richer carmine flowers and paler
markings on the leathery foliage – creating a most
beautiful effect.

Illustration: *Dactylorhiza
praetermissa*

Dactylorhiza

There are about 30 species of dactylorhiza, all tubers, in the family Orchidaceae. All genera of Orchidaceae are protected by the Convention on International Trade in Endangered Species (CITES). Responsible nurseries will propagate these plants from seed gathered in the wild. Responsible gardeners will make sure they obtain their plants *only* from such nurseries.

Dactylorhiza elata
Origin: Mediterranean
Z: 6

❧ This great marsh orchid produces spectacular flowers carried on stems that may rise as tall as 36in/90cm. The flowers appear in May or June borne on a cylindrical head up to 24in/60cm long. Each flower is exquisitely shaped, like an exotic bird in flight, deep violet purple with a darker centre and spots in the throat. In the wild it is found in damp places and in the garden it should have such a site, perhaps on the banks of a stream or pool, in an open situation or one of dappled shade. Such wild plants are best in a naturalistic setting and strikes a jarring note in an artfully contrived border.

Dactylorhiza praetermissa
Origin: N.W. Europe
Z: 6

❧ The southern marsh orchid is found in the wild in marshlands on calcareous soil. It has an imposing flowering stem rising as high as 18in/45cm crowned in June with a dazzling spike of tightly packed flowers. These are purple-red with intricate winged petals splashed with spots of deeper colour. The glaucous leaves form a handsome plumed shape at the base of the flower stem. It may be propagated by seed or by division in the early spring. This is a plant for the wilder parts of the garden. Plant it in dappled shade on the grassy bank of a stream or pool to follow primroses and cowslips.

Dahlia

There are about 30 species of dahlia, mostly tubers, in the family Compositae, all native to Central America. Apart from the one or two species described below, most garden dahlias are the highly selected hybrids of *D. coccinea* and *D. pinnata*. There are well over 400 different cultivars available commercially, and very many more have been lost to cultivation. The International Register of Dahlia Names carries the names of 20,000 cultivars. From their introduction early in the 19th century they quickly became popular. Cannell & Sons' nursery in Kent offered for sale 469 cultivars in 1890. They have remained collector's plants, with societies specialising in them, but polite garden taste has spurned them in recent times. However, with an interest in bolder schemes, their qualities are once more being recognized. Many of them provide a richness of colour and an irresistible flamboyance of flower that makes them brilliantly ornamental plants in the right setting. The National Dahlia Society of England has devised a classification based on flower shape which divides them into 31 categories, minutely defined.

The cultivars described below will start to flower in July or August and continue for many weeks, often continuing until the first winter frosts. They are tender, reliably hardy only in Zone 9. In less favoured gardens the tubers may be dug up when the first frosts have

Illustration oposite:
Dahlia 'Arabian Night'

Illustration: *Dahlia* 'Bishop of Llandaff'

blackened the top growth and then allowed to dry off in a frost-free place. They may then be stored, again in a frost-proof place, in clean soil which will prevent them from drying out entirely. When growth starts in the spring they should be transferred to richer compost before planting out when there is no danger of frost. A less laborious alternative in colder gardens, and those with heavy soil, is to keep the tubers in pots and bed them out, pot and all, in the spring, to be removed in late autumn and kept in a frost-free place.

They range very widely in colour and flower type, some are single-flowered, many are elaborately double with hundreds of petals forming a huge pompom. Some have flowers only 2in/5cm in diameter, others, especially those grown for competitions, have giant, sometimes rather absurd, flowers as much as 12in/30cm across.

D. 'Angora' is very double, white, with petals that are crimped at the tips, giving the impression of a powder puff. *D.* 'Arabian Night' has double flowers that are almost black when first open but fade slightly to a superb rich blood red. *D.* 'Bednall Beauty' has purple-bronze foliage and rich double red flowers. *D.* 'Bishop of Llandaff' (known in America as 'Japanese Bishop') is in the style of older kinds but, in fact, dates from 1928. It is a magnificent plant with strikingly

Illustration: *Dahlia*
'Chiltern Amber'

sombre purple-bronze foliage and large single flowers
of an intense scarlet with bold yellow anthers and the
texture of velvet. *D.* 'Easter Sunday' is white with
single flowers with bold yellow centres surrounded by
a secondary ruff of smaller petals. *D.* 'Yellow Hammer'
is a good pale yellow with single flowers and rounded
petals, resembling its parent *D. coccinea*. *D.* 'Chiltern
Amber' is a good rich apricot colour. But cultivars
come and go with bewildering speed and many, even
when commercially available, are to be found at only a
single nursery. It is probably best to get the catalogue
of a specialist supplier and choose the colours you need
for a particular scheme.

Dahlia coccinea
Origin: Guatemala
Z: 9

❧ This is one of the species of dahlias that have given
rise to so many of the garden cultivars. It is in itself a
magnificent garden plant, not, alas, very hardy, and can
make a tremendous contribution to the border. In its
native habitat it will grow as tall as 10ft/3m but it needs
a long hot summer and plenty of feeding and water to
do as well as that. Its flowers are large, single, a

dazzling pure scarlet with a crisp golden eye. The leaves are pinnate and the flowering stems are attractively flushed with purple. The plant has the distinctive dahlia characteristic of having hanging flower buds, looking curiously like greenish strawberries, which flop upwards when the flower opens, to present itself full face. It is magnificent among crocosmias, daylilies and other hot coloured plants. It must have sunshine and it will certainly need support.

Dahlia merckii
Origin: Mexico
Z: 8

❧ This species dahlia has none of the bravado of the large cultivars but it does have great charm and an admirably long flowering season. It will grow to 4ft/1.2m, throwing out airy branches with scattered flowers appearing from June onwards. These are single, lilac-coloured, with a yellow eye, and continue well into the autumn. It must have a sunny position in a very well-drained position. It is excellent in a mixed border where it will interweave with other plants. I have seen it used to great effect on a precipitous south-facing slope. There is a good white form, *D. merckii alba,* and an even better cultivar of it with finely pointed petals, *D. merckii* 'Hadspen Star.'

Dichelostemma

There are about six species of dichelostemma in the family Alliaceae/Liliaceae. They are all corms and native to the Western U.S.A.

Dichelostemma congestum
Origin: W. U.S.A.
Z: 8

ॐ This charming plant shows its relationship to the onion tribe. It produces its flowers in late June, a rounded umbel of warm violet flowerlets with pale lemon centres. The umbels are held on rather stiff stems which rise as high as 24in/60cm. It should have a sunny position in very well-drained soil. It may seed itself, forming a colony, and looking very decorative among the smaller shrubs which enjoy the same conditions such as artemisias, cistus, lavender, sage and santolina. Its flowers are beautiful among the dusky foliage of *Salvia officinalis* 'Purpurascens'. It may also be propagated by dividing the corms in the autumn.

Dichelostemma ida-maia
Origin: W. U.S.A.
Z: 7

The expressive common name for this cheerful plant is the firecracker flower. Its former scientific name was *Brodiaea ida-maia*. From a mass of leaves the wiry flowering stems, up to 12in/30cm tall, produce their dazzling flowers in late June. These are little crimson hanging tubes tipped with gold-green. They have a glistening texture, as though freshly painted. The flowers sway on their stems and provide brilliant spots of colour, looking especially beautiful among pale grey foliage. It must have a sunny position in well-drained soil – it will flourish in quite poor soil. It needs water in spring to develop its flowers but the corms welcome a completely dry position after flowering. It may be propagated by seed – in favourable conditions it will seed itself – or by dividing the corms in the autumn. It is an excellent plant for pots, alone or mixed with others, where it may be given precisely the conditions it demands. The corms may be lifted in the autumn and replanted in early spring in fresh compost with plenty of grit for good drainage.

Dierama

Dierama dracomontanum
Origin: South Africa
Z: 9

Dierama pulcherrimum
Origin: South Africa
Z: 7

There are over 40 species of dierama, all corms, in the family Iridaceae, native to central and southern Africa.

ஐ This dierama is one of the less hardy kinds but it is a plant of tremendous character. It forms a clump up to 36in/90cm high and produces its flowers in June on stiff stems (unlike its swaying sister described below). The flowers are loosely trumpet shaped and range in colour from pinkish red to much deeper shades. The best colour is a deep, dusty red which would be a superlative ingredient in a border of hot colours. It is best in rich soil and needs plenty of moisture at flowering time. It has a long flowering season and looks beautiful in a border of greys, reds and purple with such plants as artichokes, geraniums, penstemons and sidalceas.

ஐ The common name of this dierama, the wand flower, comes from the long, thin, swaying flower stems which rise like wands above the foliage. The flowers hang downwards on hair-like stems on which they swing gracefully. They open in June and vary in colour from pale rosy-pink to a much richer, almost magenta pink. The flowering stems will rise as high as 6ft/1.8m and the flowers are borne over several weeks. In the wild it grows in rich, moist soil and in gardens it

Illustration:
Dierama pendulum

is often planted in a sunny position on the banks of a stream or pool. In a border it is superbly ornamental, with the flowers suspended high above other plants. In rich soil it will form a substantial clump sending out generous flowering stems. The evergreen foliage is grass-like and rather scrappy and it is certainly no loss if it is concealed by other plants. It may be propagated by dividing clumps in autumn. Some particularly attractive cultivars have been bred by the Slieve Donard nursery such as *D. pulcherrimum* 'Blackbird' which has rich purple flowers. *D. pendulum* is very similar to *D. pulcherrimum* in all respects except that its petals stand out from the stems making the whole raceme fuller, forming a striking tassel.

Disporum

Disporum flavens
Origin: Korea
Z: 5

There are about 10 species of disporum, all rhizomes, in the family Convallariaceae/Liliaceae

❧ This decorative woodland plant has something of the character of a yellow-flowered Solomon's Seal (*Polygonatum*) but with distinct charm of its own. It produces its flowers in May, pale yellow hanging tubes with curiously prominent stamens which curl outwards at the tip. The flowers dangle attractively in a tuft of downward pointing leaves. The fleshy stems that carry both leaves and flowers rise about 12in/30cm high are

dark at the bottom becoming paler further up. The leaves are a fresh green, sweepingly oval with pointed tips and pronounced furrows on their surface. The leaves continue to be decorative long after the flowering is over. This is a plant for moist shade where its flower colour will associate particularly attractively with ferns that have yellow-green new foliage. It may be propagated by dividing the rhizomes in the autumn.

Dracunculus

Dracunculus vulgaris
Origin: Mediterranean
Z: 9

There are three species of dracunculus, all tuberous perennials, in the family Araceae, native to Europe.

❧ I can never quite make up my mind whether this is merely curious or actually decorative. It is certainly striking, and has handsome details, but is it garden-worthy? It is known as the dragon plant and has long been grown in gardens. Its new shoots are

Illustration opposite:
Eranthis hyemalis

attractively mottled and its foliage boldly divided, rich green with pale markings. Its flowers in summer are a splendid sight – like those of a rakish cousin of 'Lords and Ladies' (*Arum maculatum*) – deep purple spathes with undulating margins with a long, pointed, almost black spadix. The flower gives off a horrible smell, like decaying flesh. The whole plant grows to a height of about 36in/90cm. It must have a warm, sunny position and may be propagated by dividing the tubers.

Epipactis

There are over 20 species of epipactis, in the family Orchidaceae, very widely distributed in Africa, America, Europe and Asia.

Epipactis palustris
Origin: Europe
Z: 6

❧ The marsh helleborine is a late-flowering orchid which would make a lovely ornament in the wild garden. It rises to a height of about 15in/35cm with, in late summer, a spray of flowers at the tip. These are very intricate, with wings resembling insects and coloured in shades of white, yellow and pink. The stems are rather hairy with upwards pointing leaves carried alternately. In the wild it is found in damp places in acid soil. But it will tolerate slightly alkaline soil provided it has sufficient moisture. It is a marvellous plant for the edge of a stream. It may be propagated in the spring by dividing the rhizomes.

Eranthis

The name *Eranthis* comes from the Greek for spring flower. There are about seven species, in the family Ranunculaceae. They are all tuberous-rooted perennials, native to Europe, Central Asia and Japan.

Eranthis hyemalis
Origin: S. Europe
Z: 5

❧ Few plants create a livelier scene than a fine spread of the winter aconite flaunting its gleaming, cheerful yellow on a January day – in a mild winter it may even be in flower before Christmas. The single flower is at first globular but opens out into a cupped shape, 1in/2.5cm in diameter, very much resembling its cousin the meadow buttercup (*Ranunculus acris*). The flowers

Illustration: *Eranthis hyemalis* 'Guinea Gold'

rise above a decorative ruff of leaves encircling the fleshy stems which are up to 2in/5cm long holding the flowers well aloft. After the flowers have fallen the leaves continue to grow, becoming larger and rising higher, making a decorative pattern. In the wild the winter aconite flourishes in humus-rich soil, neutral or calcareous, in woodland and scrub. In the garden it will do best in a similar position. An ideal position for it is at the foot of a deciduous tree where it will form a spectacular golden carpet, getting all the moisture it needs in the winter and lying dormant in the dry summer. In the woodland garden, or in some shady bed, it is an essential partner of other winter-flowering plants – snowdrops, Lenten hellebores (*Helleborus orientalis*) and *Cyclamen coum*. The foliage of other smaller plants such as *Arum italicum* ssp. *italicum* 'Marmoratum', pulmonarias and hardy geraniums make an ornamental background. A later-flowering cultivar, *E.* 'Guinea Gold' has deeper yellow flowers, set off by a ruff of leaves flushed with bronze, and a longer-flowering season. Propagation is by division soon after flowering, but it may take time for plants to settle down and flower successfully. This is a much more reliable way of acquiring them than by buying the dried rhizomes which are sometimes offered for sale. Some failures are reported from gardeners who do not plant the rhizomes sufficiently deeply. If you acquire them 'in the green', which is best, make sure you plant them to exactly the same depth as is indicated by the plants, which will be between 2in/5cm and 3in/8cm of earth above the top of the rhizome.

Eremurus

There are about 40 species of eremurus in the family Asphodelaceae/Liliaceae.

Eremurus robustus
Origin: Afghanistan, Russia
Z: 7

❧ Few border plants combine to such a striking degree the presence and the delicacy of this lovely plant. Known as the fox-tail lily, its flower stems rise very tall, as high as 8ft/2.5m, bearing in June a long bottle-brush of flowers, sometimes as long as 4ft/1.2m. The flowerlets are the palest pink, delicately formed with prominent stamens which give the whole surface a blurred texture. The foliage is strap-like and insignificant, often withering by the time the plant is in flower. It should have a sunny site and needs fertile, light soil. In windy places the flowering stems will be deformed, twisting hither and thither. At the back of a big border, rising airily above all other herbaceous plants, it is dazzlingly lovely. It has a long flowering season. It may be propagated by division.

Eremurus stenophyllus
ssp. *stenophyllus*
Origin: Central Asia
Z: 5

❧ This is a smaller fox-tail lily than *E. robustus*. Its flowering stems rise only to 5ft/1.5m making it less prone to wind damage. It is similar in other ways but the flowers are a pale yellow becoming a warm tawny gold as they age. It is a marvellous plant for the smaller border, especially with blues and golds. It is especially beautiful against deep purple foliage such as that of *Cotinus coggygria* 'Royal Purple' or of *Corylus maxima* 'Purpurea.' It may be planted in a very large pot but it should be accompanied by other planting at its base to conceal its rather scrappy foliage.

Erythronium

There are about 20 species of erythronium, all bulbs, in the family Liliaceae/Liliaceae native to North America, Europe and, a single species only, Japan. They are found in a very wide range of habitats from moist woodland to dry mountainsides. The name comes from the Greek for red which is the colour of the flowers of the native European *Erythronium dens-canis*. Some of the west-coast North American species are known in the U.S.A. as trout lilies and some, indeed, have leaf-markings that resemble the scales of a fish sparkling underwater. Although they vary in habitat they may all be propagated by dividing clumps of bulbs as the leaves die and replanting in enriched soil. In most gardens the best months will be June or July; in dry weather make sure that the new site is well watered. The colours of flowers and the markings of the foliage will vary within a particular species.

Erythronium americanum
Origin: Eastern North America
Z: 3

❧ This little erythronium has flowers that resemble miniature elongated daffodils of a lovely pale lemon yellow. The leaves are long and pleated down the middle, marked with handsome marbling of brown and grey. The flowers, which appear in April, are held on tall stems 4in/10cm high which curl over at the top. In its native America it is a plant of woodland and pastures and in the garden it looks beautiful in dappled woodland shade growing in rich moist humus among, for example, moss and wood anemones. Although the bulbs are quite small they should be planted fairly deeply – no less than 5in/12.5cm. Despite the delicacy of its appearance it is among the more robust of the erythroniums. Its great charm is the combination of sharp yellow with the simple form of its flowers rising above distinguished foliage. There are flashier plants but few more beautiful.

Erythronium californicum
Origin: California
Z: 5

❧ This Californian erythronium grows in the wild in coniferous woods. It has striking flowers, opening in April from creamy pink buds. When the petals curve back they reveal a cream-yellow interior with protruding pale anthers. The interior is worth looking at – the base of the throat is marked with deep purple 'sight lines' to guide bees about their fertilizing business. Up to three flowers are borne on the tip of each stem which is dusky purple in colour and rises to a

height of 12in/30cm. The leaves are especially
attractive, a pale glistening green handsomely marked
with paler marbling. They are rather more erect than in
many erythroniums and form a decorative sheaf from
which the flowering stems emerge. In the garden it will
grow well in shade or part shade, performing best in
rich but well-drained soil. *E. citrinum*, from California
and Oregon, is very similar but with a sharper yellow
to its colouring. 'White Beauty' is either a cultivar of
E. californicum or a hybrid. It is more vigorous and
very beautiful, forming generous clumps with the same
decorative markings. The flowers have less yellow and
are larger than the type. I grow it successfully in the
shade, against a north-facing wall among the foliage of
Cyclamen hederifolium.

Erythronium dens-canis
Origin: Asia, Europe
Z: 3

❧ The dog's-tooth violet – which is not a violet at all –
takes its name from the curious shape of the bulb
which slightly resembles a large, elongated tooth. It is
the only native European erythronium and an
exceptionally decorative plant. Its foliage is very
striking, each leaf up to 3in/8cm long, rounded and
pointed, and marked with deep purple marbling on a
lively green background. The flowers, which open in
March – the earliest of the erythroniums – are a
sprightly purple-pink, trumpet shaped and at first
downward pointing on curved stems. When they are

fully open the petals sweep backwards revealing long pale stamens tipped with dramatic purple anthers. In the sun the colour of the flower will fade to a rosy pink. In the wild the dog's-tooth violet grows in woodland and meadows. In the garden it will flourish in the same sort of conditions that are best for cyclamen and hellebores – moist soil in part shade. After the flowers have faded the leaves will grow with greater vigour, making bold clumps and overlapping to form a lively pattern. The foliage looks splendid intermingled with that of *Cyclamen hederifolium*. There are several named cultivars few of which improve on the type and some of which are positively coarse and overblown – 'Pink Perfection', for example. A white variety, *E. dens-canis* 'White Splendour', has much charm, retaining the dark violet centre of the type.

Erythronium helenae
Origin: California
Z: 5

❧ The combination of highly decorative foliage and sparkling flowers makes this one of the finest erythroniums. Its flowers open in April, creamy white but with a rich lemon-yellow centre. They are held on dark brown stems 5in/8cm high which rise above exceptionally beautiful leaves. They are long, undulating and relatively narrow, marked with smudges of maroon-chocolate, and often crisply edged with the same colour. In the garden it should have a partly-shaded site in well-drained but humus-rich soil – it will not flourish in very heavy soil that retains moisture in the winter. I have seen it looking marvellous in the dappled shade of *Magnolia stellata* whose flowers will appear at the same time – the pure white contrasting with the cream and yellow of the erythronium.

Erythronium hendersonii
Origin: N.W. North America
Z: 5

🌿 There is no such thing as an ugly erythronium – this is an especially beautiful one. It flowers in April, with the flowers on slender stems carried well above the handsomely mottled foliage. The downward-curving flower buds are a rich rosy-purple but when they open they are much paler, with the petals fading almost to white at the base. The petals separate and curve backwards throwing the purple anthers into prominence. It will bear as many as ten flowers on each stem, up to 10in/25cm high, and the contrast of colour between bud and flower makes a lively sight. In its native California and Oregon it grows in clearings in pine woods. In the garden it needs part shade and very sharp drainage in a site that allows it to be almost completely dry when dormant. The front of a sunny border, among the sprawling branches of low-growing shrubs of Mediterranean character, such as cistus or sage, would suit it well.

Erythronium
multiscapoideum
Origin: California
Z: 5

❧ From the hills of the Sierra Nevada this little erythronium is a tough customer, despite its delicate appearance. Its flowers in April are creamy white of a silken texture with well-separated petals which twist as the flower ages. The centre of the flower is a striking lemon yellow. Several flowers are borne on each plant and they rise well above the foliage carried on slender brown stems. The flowers face outwards resembling diminutive narcissi. The leaves are narrow, undulating and finely mottled with brown markings. This is a plant for the woodland garden in a position of light shade where it will make one of the loveliest ornamental plantings you could have.

Erythronium revolutum
Origin: W. N. America
Z: 5

❧ In the wild this erythronium flourishes in moist coniferous woodland, its pale pink flowers glowing in the half-light. It is variable in colour, some plants have almost white flowers but others have a much deeper pink. The flowers are especially graceful, the buds drooping elegantly before unfurling and bending their petals backwards. The petals of those plants with deeper colouring show much darker veins along their

backs. The foliage is of the trout lily kind, undulating and strikingly marked with aqueous marbling, chocolate-maroon against almost jade green. In the garden it will flower in March or April and in conditions close to its natural habitat will naturalise easily. At Knightshayes Court in Devon a particularly good rich pink form, named 'Knightshayes Pink', has established a vast colony under old trees. These deeper pink clones are known collectively as the 'Johnsonii Group'. *E. revolutum* flourishes in the same conditions as bluebells (*Hyacinthoides non-scripta*) with which the dark pink kinds, flowering at the same time, will make a resplendent mixture.

Erythronium tuolumnense
Origin: California
Z: 5

❧ Among the first erythroniums in flower – often out in the middle of March in southern England – *E. tuolumnense* has a character all of its own. Its flower buds are green-gold on the outside and open into downward-hanging lemon-yellow trumpets which eventually open almost flat, like a little wild daffodil. They are smaller than other erythroniums and the petals never curve fully backwards as they do in most other kinds. Up to three flowers are carried on each stem which rises to 8in/12.5cm high. The foliage is pale green, with a shining surface, and an upwards habit of growth forming a distinguished background for the flowers. In the wild it grows on acid soil in woodland.

Illustration opposite:
Eucomis bicolor 'Alba'

Illustration:
Erythronium 'Pagoda'

In the garden it will do best in part-shade in
humus-rich soil. Plant it with other shade-loving plants
of striking foliage such as *Arum italicum* ssp. *italicum*
'Marmoratum'. *E.* 'Pagoda' is a hybrid with an
unknown white-flowered species that is more vigorous
than *E. tuolumnense*. Its stems rise higher – up to
15in/35cm – and it will produce several flowers on each
one. The flowers are of a paler yellow and the petals are
narrower and curve backwards in more characteristic
erythronium fashion.

Eucomis

There are about 10 species of eucomis, all bulbs, in
the family Hyacinthaceae/Liliaceae. They are
known as pineapple lilies from the tuft of foliage at the
top of the flowers which does indeed make them
resemble pineapples. The name eucomis is derived from
the Greek for 'beautiful hair.'

Eucomis bicolor
Origin: South Africa
Z: 8

❧ This marvellously decorative plant is rarely seen but
is increasingly available in specialist nurseries. From a
mound of gleaming, undulating strap-like leaves the
fleshy, spotted stems, rising to 18in/45cm high, produce
their exotic flowers in July. These consist of a
bottle-brush of flowerlets, deep red and lime green,

crowned with a flamboyant tuft of lime-green leaves. Like most of the eucomis tribe they give off a horrible smell, not unlike rotting meat, and attractive to flies. The flowers last for weeks, well into September. It should be planted a good 6in/15cm deep in a well-protected position that gets plenty of sun. It needs soil that is both rich and well-drained. It makes an especially distinguished pot plant, either alone or as the dramatic centrepiece of a mixed planting. It may be propagated by seed or by dividing the bulbs in late autumn. *E. bicolor* 'Alba' is a cultivar with pale lime-green flowers and no spots on the flowering stem.

Eucomis comosa
Origin: South Africa
Z: 8

❧ This stately eucomis, previously known as *E. punctata*, throws out flowering stems that rise as high as 30in/75cm erupting from handsome gleaming foliage. The flowers, which open in July or August, are variable in colour from creamy pink to purple. One authority describes their scent as 'coconut ice, elderflower and jasmine' – a heady cocktail. It has an exceptionally long flowering season, often lasting well into October. Some forms have especially attractive leaves flushed with purple. As an architectural plant, of exquisite detail, this is one of the finest late-flowering bulbs, performing at a time when few other plants can equal its exotic beauty. If you can find the right place in a border – with plenty of sun and rich, moist soil – it will give tremendous pleasure and mix easily with other plants. Failing that, it is a marvellous plant for a large pot or for use as a most exotic bedding plant.

Fritillaria

The fritillaries are among the most irresistible of bulbous plants. There are about 100 species, in the family Liliaceae/Liliaceae, very widely distributed in the temperate regions of the western hemisphere. For owners of small gardens they make an admirable subject to collect – some of the trickier kinds may be grown in troughs or pots and given precisely the conditions they require.

Fritillaria acmopetala
Origin: Asia,
Mediterranean
Z: 7

This fritillary is among the most elegant of its tribe. Its flowers appear in May, downward hanging bells whose petals curl back sharply at their tips. They are most strikingly coloured, alternate petals pale green and purple-brown. The flowers are carried at the tips of slender stems up to 10in/25cm high with wavy pale green leaves arranged alternately along the stem. In the wild it grows in clearings in woodland and in pastures. In the garden it will flourish in rich light soil in dappled shade. It would be well worth trying in a meadow garden where its relatively tall stems would give it great presence.

Fritillaria assyriaca
Origin: Turkey
Z: 8

The flowers of this fritillary are bell-shaped, hanging gracefully downwards on the tips of arched stems up to 12in/30cm high. They are deep maroon in colour, gradually fading into yellow towards the tips of the petals and the whole flower has a dusty sheen to it. The foliage is a fresh green, rising taller than the

Illustration opposite:
Fritillaria imperialis
'Maxima Lutea'

Illustration:
Fritillaria assyriaca

flowering stems. In the wild it grows in poor, stony soil in exposed places as high as 8,000ft/2,500m. In the garden, where it will flower in March or April, it must have a sunny site and very well drained soil. Its colouring associates particularly well with pale grey foliage of plants such as the narrow-leafed *Salvia lavandulifolia* which needs similar growing conditions.

Fritillaria camschatcensis
Origin: N. E. Asia, W. North America, Japan
Z: 4

❦ This is a beautiful fritillary whose flower colour varies considerably. The flowers open in May, grouped together at the tips of fleshy pale green stems which rise to about 12in/30cm. Up to six flowers are carried on each stem and they are downward hanging, rather stubby, bell-shaped with the petals opening out gracefully at their tips. They vary in colour from grey-purple, resembling slate, to a marvellous black-purple. They have bright yellow anthers. The leaves, ribbed and of a fresh green, are carried in whorls about the stem. It is a plant of woodland and meadows. In the garden it will do best in peaty soil in a position that is at least part-shaded.

Fritillaria imperialis
Origin: Asia
Z: 4

❦ The crown imperial is the largest and most spectacular of the fritillaries – growing as tall as 5ft/1.5m. From the moment its fresh green growth erupts from the soil in February to its dramatic flowering some six weeks later it is one of most

Illustration:
Fritillaria imperialis

ornamental of garden plants. Even before its growth
emerges its presence is made known by its distinct foxy
smell which many gardeners hate. I find it irresistibly
attractive, one of the most evocative scents of spring.
The foliage is a gleaming green, with leaves twisting
decoratively about the fleshy purple-brown stem. The
flowers are held in a group of up to five disposed about
the stem, hanging downwards, and crowned by a
dashing tuft of pointed leaves. They are red or
orange-red, with striking veining in a deeper colour.
They never open out fully but remain tubular and
always pointing down. But it is worth raising a flower
to peer at the dazzling interior with crystal drops of
nectar held in suspension at the bases of petals and
curious hinged anthers. Equally beautiful in all respects
is the pale yellow-flowered cultivar, *F. imperialis*
'Maxima Lutea'. There are other curiosities such as one
with variegated foliage, *F. imperialis* 'Aureomarginata',

and one with two tiers of flowers, *F. imperialis* 'Prolifera'.

As the crown imperial is such an exceptional garden plant, and one which will settle down and naturalise in appropriate conditions, it is worth taking trouble to cultivate it well. It will flourish in rich soil in sun or semi-shade. I grow it underneath the deciduous ornamental tree *Amelanchier canadensis* whose pink-flushed buds are just breaking as the crown imperials' flowers appear. It must have rich, fertile soil that never dries out. The bulb should be planted no less than 6in/15cm deep. In heavy soil it is best to put a layer of coarse grit at the bottom of the hole. The bulb is very large and has an indentation at the top which, if planted upright, will allow water to gather and rot the bulb which should, therefore, be planted on its side. It will need feeding in later life – a thick mulch of compost before the leaves appear is beneficial. Foliar feeding after the flowers have faded will also build up strength.

Fritillaria meleagris
Origin: Europe
Z: 4

❧ The snake's head fritillary has curious lantern-shaped flowers in April. They hang downwards and are a rich maroon in colouring, attractively chequered. Each petal is ribbed in a deeper colour and tipped with gold. In any community of flowers some are white with greenish markings. They are held on stems up to 12in/30cm high, a pale glaucous grey with alternate bending leaves. In nature they are found in moist meadow land and in the garden they need a position in sun or light shade where the soil does not dry out in the summer. They are at their most beautiful as part of a mixed spring planting with bluebells (*Hyacinthoides non-scripta*), daffodils and wood anemone (*Anemone nemorosa*) in long grass. They will seed themselves and naturalise rapidly in conditions that suit them. The quickest method of building up a community is to gather seed and sow it in trays, transplanting the seedlings when large enough.

Fritillaria michailovskyi
Origin: Turkey
Z: 7

❧ This little fritillary, no more than 6in/15cm in height, has flowers of dazzling colouring. They hanging downwards, loosely bell-shaped, swaying on their stems. The upper part of the flower is very deep maroon, almost chocolate-coloured, with a dusty texture and the rims of the petals are rich yellow, forming a bold band at the mouth. A well-established colony gives off a delicious scent of honey. It needs a warm, sunny site and is best in well-drained soil – if your soil is heavy it is essential to add grit. In its native habitat it is found in mountainous regions up to 10,000ft/3,000m and flowers in the summer. In temperate lowland areas it will flower in the early spring and is best in a site that is hot and dry in the summer. A position in front of smaller shrubs, such as sages, will suit it well. The purple-leafed sage *Salvia officinalis* 'Purpurascens' makes a striking foil for the flowers.

Fritillaria pallidiflora
Origin: Central Asia
Z: 3

❧ This is one of the best fritillaries for the woodland garden, with marvellous presence and distinction in all its details. In its native habitat it is found in shady places in mountainous regions. It has handsome pale glaucous foliage, wide and pointed and elegantly curved. The flowers in April or May are carried well above the foliage, hanging in groups of three from the tips of stems which rise 12in/30cm high. Each flower is a hanging bell with shapely petals, a pale creamy-yellow and sometimes flushed with pink. Petals are strikingly marked with an intricate pattern of veins and the flowers give off a curious musky scent. It is at its best in a shady position in rich, peaty soil. It is a wonderful companion for wood anemones.

Fritillaria persica
Origin: Iran, Turkey
Z: 5

❧ The Persian fritillary is one of the most dramatically beautiful of the genus. It rises to a height of 4ft/1.2m and its stems are crowned in April by tall spires of hanging, bell-shaped flowers. They are dusty purple in colour, with lemon yellow anthers making a sharp

contrast. Although fairly tough (in the wild it flourishes in mountainous country at heights of up to 8,000ft/2,500m) in the garden it needs rich soil and a position in full sun. The foliage is handsome, with broad grey-green leaves emerging horizontally from the stem. The cultivar *F. persica* 'Adiyaman' has much darker maroon, almost black, flowers. It makes an excellent plant for a pot.

Fritillaria pyrenaica
Origin: France, Spain
Z: 5

❧ This fritillary from the meadows of the Pyrenees is like a splendidly distinguished cousin of the snake's head fritillary, *Fritillaria meleagris*. It grows to a height of 12in/30cm and flowers in April or May. The flowers are pale yellow strikingly marked with a purple-brown chequerboard pattern on the backs of the petals. The shape of the flower is distinctive with rather square 'shoulders' at the top and recurved tips to the petals. The flowering stem is glaucous green with wispy leaves arranged alternately up the stem. It is found in the wild as high as 7,000ft/2,000m and in the garden makes a superb ingredient for a cultivated meadow or in dappled shade at the edge of woodland. There is also a very beautiful almost pure yellow form.

Fritillaria raddeana
Origin: SW Central Asia
Z: 4

❧ This is like a smaller, much simplified version of *Fritillaria imperialis* with which it shares that curious, foxy smell. It grows to a height of 18in/45cm and bears its flowers in groups with a tuft of leaves rising above. The flowers are single, of the palest creamy-yellow, hanging downwards and spreading elegantly sideways when fully open. The leaves are a glistening, pale green, and twist decoratively. The fleshy stems are slightly flushed with purple. It is very hardy but flowers early in the year – in a mild season as early as February. Thus it may need some protection and may be best in the alpine house or bulb frame. I am experimenting with growing it in a very sunny border, backed by a stone wall, with a background of the glaucous foliage of *Euphorbia characias* ssp. *wulfenii*.

Illustration opposite:
Galanthus nivalis

Galanthus

There are about fourteen species of snowdrop, all native to Europe, in the family Amaryllidaceae/ Liliaceae, but many of these are very changeable and there are as many as 600 cultivars. Snowdrops have been taken up by collectors many of whom look out for minute variations – such as the markings on the petals – that make little difference to the garden-worthiness of the plant. All species prefer a moist soil, neutral or alkaline, and a position in partial shade – many will flourish in complete shade. All those described below are winter flowering, in temperate places in a mild winter they will flower in January. The species *G. reginae-olgae*, scarcely distinguishable to the gardener's eye from the common *G. nivalis*, flowers in the autumn when I think it looks completely out of season. To me these are the quintessential bulbs of the winter looking marvellous with other bulbous plants that flower at the same time such as aconites (*Eranthis hyemalis*) and *Cyclamen coum*, and with the decorative foliage of emerging pulmonarias, hardy geraniums and *Arum italicum* ssp. *italicum* 'Marmoratum'. Colonies of them under deciduous trees – which often provide the perfect habitat – are a superlative winter ornament. They may be propagated by division of clumps which is best done as the leaves begin to wither.

Illustration: *Galanthus elwesii* 'Flore Pleno'

Galanthus elwesii
Origin: The Balkans
Z: 6

❧ This Balkan snowdrop is like a much larger cousin of *G. nivalis*. Its foliage is broad and strap-like, up to 12in/30cm tall, and the flowers are more substantial. There is a good double form *G. elwesii* 'Flore Pleno'. This is a snowdrop of commanding presence, holding its own in decorative impact with ferns, hellebores and the emerging foliage of herbaceous plants.

Galanthus nivalis
Origin: Europe
Z: 4

❧ *Galanthus nivalis* is the common snowdrop native or naturalised in many parts of Europe. It is an irresistibly elegant and attractive little plant, one of the few plants that all gardeners will want to possess. The leaves are very slender and the flowers in January or February, up to 3/4in/2cm in length, are carried on stems 4–5in/10–12.5cm long. The flowers hang downwards, with petals slightly separate. A double form *G. nivalis* 'Flore Pleno' is also attractive. *G.* 'S. Arnott', of uncertain derivation but related to *G. nivalis*, is very vigorous, with more rounded flowers which have a strong honey scent.

Galtonia

There are four species of galtonia in the family Hyacinthaceae/Liliaceae. They are all bulbous and native to southern Africa.

Galtonia candicans
Origin: South Africa
Z: 5

The summer hyacinth, as it sometimes called, is a prince among late summer-flowering bulbs. In late July or August it unfurls its splendid flowers. A tall, fleshy stem, glaucous green, up to 36in/90cm high, is crowned by a spire of hanging bell-like flowers, creamy white with a green base, looking like those of a giant and aristocratic cousin of the spring snowflake (*Leucojum*). The broad strap-like leaves with a lustrous surface form a handsome base to the stems. It must have rich, moist soil, in a sunny position, where it will settle down and seed. As a versatile bulb for the border it has few rivals in this season. It will go easily with almost any other planting but I have seen it in a Scottish garden looking magnificent planted in quantity among pale apricot coloured lilies. In cold gardens, it makes an excellent plant for a large container. It may be propagated by seed or by removing bulbils.

Galtonia princeps
Origin: South Africa
Z: 8

❧ This rather tender galtonia, smaller than *G. candicans* described above, is easy to overlook in the jumble of a border but the more it is studied the more irresistible it appears. Its flowering stem, up to 24in/60cm tall, bears a bold tuft of flower buds, like a giant plump ear of wheat without the whiskers. The individual flowers open in July, small pistachio-green trumpets, opening out at the tips with pointed petals. It must have rich, moist soil and a sunny position. Try and find a place where its subtle character will not be swamped by the more obvious charms of flashier plants. It may be propagated by seed or by removing bulbils. It looks wonderful rising above pale cream eschscholzias. *Galtonia viridiflora* has a similar colour of flowers, with a touch of yellow, which are held in looser, more elongated and taller spires.

Galtonia regalis
Origin: South Africa
Z: 8

❧ In many ways this rare galtonia is the finest of them all. In August it throws out 36in/90cm curving flower stems from which the flowers are suspended. It does not make such a well-defined flower-head as *G. candicans*, the flowers being more separate and well distributed along the stem. Each flower is a hanging bell, the colour of the flesh of a ripe avocado. It has the

most decorative foliage of all the galtonias. Strap-like, a good 3in/8cm broad, a beautiful lustrous lime green, the leaves curve hither and thither at the base of the flowering stems creating a lively effect. There is a sparkling freshness about the whole plant which makes one think more of the spring than the sultry days of late summer. It must have a sunny position in sharply drained soil and it will look superlative among the smaller shrubs that enjoy a similar position – cistus, lavenders, sages or santolina.

Geranium

Most species of geranium, of which there about 300 in the family Geraniaceae, are herbaceous, or slightly woody, perennials. The one described here is unique in the genus because it is tuberous.

Geranium tuberosum
Origin: Mediterranean
Z: 8

&❧ This is among the first geraniums to flower, towards the beginning of May. Its flowers are a cheerful rich violet with silken petals crisply veined in a much deeper colour. It has very fine foliage with intricately cut

leaves which form striking hummocks about 8in/20cm high. It must have a sunny position and will flower well in quite poor soil. In the right position it will scatter seed liberally and form a self-perpetuating colony. It is an excellent plant for the front of a border intermingled perhaps with pinks whose pale grey foliage makes a good background for the sharp colour of the geranium's flowers.

Gladiolus

The modern florist's gladiolus is derived from hybrids of several South African species but these are not hardy in European gardens. However, there are some species, or cultivars close to them, that are hardy and make admirable garden plants. There are in all about 200 species, all corms, in the family Iridaceae.

Gladiolus callianthus
Origin: Tropical Africa
Z: 9

❧ Also known as *Acidanthera murielae* this very attractive gladiolus is tender but I have found that it is a very easy pot plant and the corms multiply obligingly with little trouble. It puts out stiff blade-like foliage above which the flowering stems rise to a height of about 36in/90cm. The flowers appear in August or September, dazzling white with spreading pointed petals and marked with a deep purple splodge in the throat. They are deliciously scented, with a hint of almonds. I have grown it in a large pot where it makes a marvellous ornament on a terrace. The corms are quite small and may be packed in 2in/5cm apart. The pots will need plenty of watering up to flowering time and, when the foliage has died away, the corms should be dried out and kept in a frost-free place. In spring they should be potted in new compost and may be started off in a cool greenhouse which will encourage early growth. In sheltered gardens it would be worth trying it in a very sunny position in well-drained soil, planting the corms a good 5in/12.5cm deep.

Gladiolus communis ssp. *byzantinus*
Origin: Mediterranean
Z: 6

❧ The Byzantine gladiolus is one of the most exotic plants that will naturalise easily – almost invasively – in temperate gardens. It has stiff blade-like leaves above which the flowering stems – 24in/60cm high – are tipped with groups of flower buds, flushed with bronze, that curve over like the beak of some strange bird. As the buds swell they take on a more pronounced purple colour with a decorative bloom, opening out at the end of May into splendid, outrageous magenta trumpets with white stripes in their throats. There are, in fact, two colours in the flowers – crimson and a purple which has an iridescent sheen; the two intermingle to appear as a single colour. It will seed itself benignly in the garden, scattering its dazzling colour in odd corners. It may also be propagated by detaching the cormlets that are formed at the base. It does well in poor, thin soil but must have a sunny position. In our garden it has dashing presence in a mixture of love-in-the-mist, *Nigella damascena*, and columbines, *Aquilegia communis,* which include the pink and white flowered 'Norah Barlow'. It is also an excellent plant for a purple and red border – rising above the sombre purple of the shrubby *Salvia purpurascens* or intermingled with the rose-pink *Cistus purpureus*. The emphatic foliage is always decorative, giving crisp architectural form in a border.

Gladiolus papilio
Origin: South Africa
Z: 8

The smaller species gladiolus are plants whose attractions gardeners should explore more deeply. The leaves of *G. papilio* (also known as *G. purpureo-auratus*) are narrow, upright, of a striking pale glaucous grey. The flowers open in August, long pointed buds, rosy-purple smudged with lime-green, several borne on the wiry, arching stems. When the flowers open fully a yellow interior is visible. The flower stems rise

24in/60cm but are bowed down by the weight of the flowers which sway prettily on their slender stems. It should have a sunny position and it needs moisture to flower well – a fairly rich but well-drained soil suits it perfectly. In suitable conditions it will spread swiftly – in some lucky gardens becoming almost invasive. It is marvellous at the front of a border threading its way through low-growing shrubs. It is said to flower more profusely if it is constricted in a pot. I have seen it looking beautiful rising above a clump of *Zauschneria californica* which produces its vermilion flowers at the same time.

Gladiolus 'The Bride'
Origin: Garden
Z: 8

❧ This is among the most elegant of the smaller gladiolus. It produces its flowers in May or June, crisply white, shaped like an irregular wide-open trumpet with pointed petals. At the base of the petals the white merges into lime green giving the whole flower a sparklingly fresh appearance. The flower stems rise 24in/60cm, and are rather stiff and thus do not need staking. The corms should be planted 6in/15cm deep in well-drained but rich soil. A sunny position is essential. In mild years the leaves will often emerge in early spring and be vulnerable to frost. A light mulch of something like mushroom compost will protect them. It makes a superlative plant for pots. It is propagated by dividing the corms in the spring.

Hedychium

The ginger lilies are a genus of about 40 species in the family Zingiberaceae, rhizomatous perennials native to the tropics.

Hedychium coronarium
Origin: India
Z: 9

❧ This is one of the less tender hedychiums and makes a wonderfully ornamental exotic plant. The leaves are magnificent, 24in/60cm long, with a lustrous surface. The flowers in late summer or early autumn are white, gathered together in a bold spike, with a delicious, sweet scent. In its native habitat *H. coronarium* comes from very moist areas and may be grown standing in water. At the very least it will need rich, moist soil in the sunniest, most protected position you can find. Few gardeners have experimented with the hardiness of these magnificent species. They make marvellous plants for a large container or they may be treated as summer bedding plants where they are a superb ingredient for an exotic scheme. There are several available commercially. *H. densiflorum* (Zone 8) has orange flowers and *H. gardnerianum* (Zone 9) has yellow flowers and particularly handsome large leaves. They are easy to propagate by dividing the rhizomes in the spring.

Hemerocallis

The daylilies are one of the most valuable, and easiest, of border plants. Their name comes from the Greek words for 'day' and 'beauty', a reference to the short life of each flower. There are about 15 species, all rhizomes, in the family Hemerocallidaceae/Liliaceae, all native to East Asia, China and Japan. Large numbers of cultivars have been bred in recent years, many from America. Over 20,000 cultivar names have been registered some of which are lovely garden plants but all too often the character of the whole plant has been sacrificed for gaudy and outlandish flowers which are sometimes of absurdly disproportionate size. Some of the names alone are enough to discourage the gardener – could you learn to love something called 'Little Fat Dazzler'? I describe in detail below some of the species. But the following modern cultivars are very

Illustration opposite:
Hemerocallis 'Golden Chimes'

Illustration:
Hemerocallis fulva

good: 'American Revolution' is early flowering with dark red flowers of velvet texture and elegantly tapered form; 'Claudine' is rich red with a darker eye, a marvellous ingredient of 'hot' schemes; 'Golden Chimes', one of the oldest cultivars, is early flowering with elegant small flowers, rich yellow within and marked with golden-brown on the backs of the petals; 'Helle Berlineren' has striking pale pink-cream flowers in June; 'Stafford' is for bold gardeners only – it has dazzling scarlet flowers in June with a white rib. Daylily cultivars come and go with great rapidity. As with dahlias the best advice is to study the stock of a specialist supplier and order colours and shapes to suit your scheme. There are increasing numbers of dwarf varieties which are both compact in height – as low as 12in/30cm – as well as having flowers in proportion, sometimes as small as 2 1/2in/6cm in diameter. These exist in a wide range of colours and are valuable for small gardens.

All daylilies need moist, rich soil and will benefit from foliar feeding from the moment their leaves emerge in the spring until the flower buds are formed. A sunny position will produce the most floriferous plants. They may be propagated by dividing clumps in late summer or autumn. Species may be propagated by seed but with seed gathered in the garden there will usually be some loss of identity.

Hemerocallis citrina
Origin: China
Z: 4

This daylily has sharp yellow flowers, deliciously scented. The flowers opening from June onwards last for several weeks and are up to 4in/10cm long, with well-separated petals which some garden authorities criticise for being too stiff. The petals are saved from too much rigidity by having attractively undulating edges. I think of them as being crisply defined and therefore having great presence in a mixed planting. It will make a compact clump, rising to 30in/75cm. Yellow is a difficult colour in the garden and this is one of the best. Graham Thomas called it the commuter's daylily because it did not open until the evening – a slight exaggeration, but it is certainly not an early riser.

Hemerocallis fulva 'Green Kwanso'
Origin: Japan
Z: 4

❧ This exotic daylily was formerly known as *H.* 'Kwanso Flore Pleno'. Its flowers, which appear in July and flower for several weeks, are flamboyant both in colour and form. They are orange coloured and suffused with yellow, with a semi-double arrangement of petals. The outer petals curl backwards, thrusting the inner ones out. Some of the petals have smooth edges, others are frilled and undulating. There is nothing soothing about these flowers, they are full of excitement and vibrating with colour. They are carried at the tips of substantial stems that rise to a height of 36in/90cm. They come into their own in a bold colour scheme and I have seen them magnificently used in bold clumps among the deepest red dahlias and the soaring orange spotted flowers of *Lilium pardalinum* with crimson double-flowered nasturtiums lapping at their feet. The single *H. fulva*, one of the oldest daylilies in gardens, is a plant of great distinction with petals alternately coloured pale apricot and pale orange-brown.

Illustration opposite:
Hemerocallis fulva 'Green Kwanso'

Hemerocallis lilioasphodelus
Origin: Japan
Z: 4

❧ This lovely daylily was formerly known as *H. flava*. It is among the earlier flowering kinds, producing its flowers in June. These are exquisitely shaped, wide open trumpets, like a very exotic daffodil. They are pale lemon yellow with a delicious, sweet scent. The stems, which are very slender, rise 30in/75cm tall. It will flower well in sun or in

part-shade – it is especially lovely in the dappled shade under a light canopy of leaves. The refinement of this daylily puts to shame so many coarse and overblown cultivars. It is a beautiful plant for the border, looking lovely with pale blue delphiniums.

Hemerocallis middendorfii
Origin: Asia
Z: 5

❧ This shows all the distinction of the best species daylilies. It flowers early in June, single lemon yellow trumpets with a marvellous scent. The petals curve backwards, making a flower of the greatest elegance. The plant is very upright with striking presence, the flowers borne on stiff stems up to 24in/60cm high among slender rush-like leaves. It is admirable with blues such as the silver-blue of *Geranium pratense* 'Mrs Kendall Clark' and the violet of *Viola cornuta*. It also goes well with the lime-green flowers of *Euphorbia characias* ssp. *wulfenii*.

Hermodactylus

There is only one species of hermodactylus, in the family Iridaceae.

Hermodactylus tuberosus
Origin: S. Europe
Z: 7

❧ Also known as the snake's head or widow iris, this lovely tuber is among the most decorative of all bulbous plants flowering in its season. The sweetly scented flowers open in April or May, iris-like, carried at the tips of stems 10in/25cm long. They are the colour of yellow Chartreuse but the falls are black, with the texture of velvet. In my own heavy clay, and plagued by slugs, it is a difficult plant. It is better in lighter, well-drained soil where it may seed itself prolifically. It should be planted in a sunny position or in part shade. In the garden it needs a simple setting, where it will not be overshadowed by plants of coarser charms. It is beautiful rising behind the pale green new foliage of *Alchemilla mollis*. It may be propagated by dividing clumps in autumn.

Hyacinthoides

There are four species, all annual bulbs, in the family Hyacinthaceae/Liliaceae, all native to Europe and N. Africa.

Hyacinthoides non-scripta
(syn. *Scilla non-scripta*)
Origin: Europe
Z: 5

❧ The common bluebell should only be planted in a naturalistic setting – in a formal bed it looks absurd. It is found in the wild in beech or oak woodland and anyone who has ever seen it flowering in April, spreading a smoky blue carpet through the trees, will

Illustration opposite:
Bluebells (*Hyacinthcoides non-scripta*) in an English wood

recognise that nature had the best idea for its ideal position. The flowers are carried at the tips of fleshy stems, 12in/30cm tall, a mid blue with a hint of violet. Each flower is a diminutive bell, with petals curving back at the tip, hanging in clusters on one side of the stem. Occasional white forms are found and a much less desirable wishy-washy pink. In gardens it may cross with the undistinguished Spanish bluebell, *H. hispanica*, to produce prolific but dull offspring. The true bluebell must be planted on a grand scale – do not consider it if you have only a small garden. In woodland it will associate beautifully with substantial ornamental shrubs.

Ipheion

The name of this genus has been kicked about by botanists – it has been known under *Tristagma* and *Triteleia*. There are ten species of bulbous plants in the family Alliaceae/Liliaceae, all of which are native to South America.

Illustration: *Ipheion uniflorum* 'Wisley Blue'

Ipheion uniflorum
Origin: Argentina, Uruguay
Z: 6

❧ The spring starflower is one of those valuable small plants, very undemanding as to site, which will ornament all sorts of odd corners in the garden. It forms a hummock of fresh green strap-like leaves – with a powerful scent of onion. The flowers appear in February or March, borne at the tip of 6in/10cm stems,

each flower 1 1/2in/4cm across, star-shaped with pointed petals. They are pale blue with a deeper line down the centre of each petal, both front and back, and lemon-yellow stamens. The flowers have the faint but clear smell of honey, much magnified in the sun. In my own garden *Ipheion uniflorum* forms handsome clumps and it will flower well in semi-shade or in full sun, scattering itself obligingly. It looks beautiful with some of the pale yellows of other spring-flowering plants. I have seen it with the creamy-yellow double primrose *Primula vulgaris alba* 'Alba Plena'. It also makes a good plant for a pot, with its abundant foliage forming a fringe about the edge. It is very easily propagated by division of clumps. Some good cultivars are available, among them *I.uniflorum* 'Froyle Mill' with richer violet-blue flowers; *I. uniflorum* 'Wisley Blue', with strong blue flowers; and *I.uniflorum* 'Rolf Fiedler' with pale blue flowers with a striking white centre. *I. uniflorum album* is a good pure white form.

Iris

There are over 200 species of iris, in the family Iridaceae, widely distributed, but only in the temperate regions of the northern hemisphere. There are well over 800 cultivars commercially available in Britain, varying enormously in size and in colour – the name comes from Iris, the messenger in Greek

Illustration:
Pacific Coast iris

mythology who descended from the heavens in a
rainbow. They are all rhizomes or bulbs and may be
divided broadly into bearded and beardless kinds. The
bearded sorts, all of which are rhizomes, have a patch
of fuzz on the inside of the 'fall' – the downward-
curving petal which gives so many irises their especially
graceful character. It is from the species bearded irises
(such as the European native *I. variegata*) that the
majority of garden cultivars have been bred. There has
been a frenzy of iris breeding, with new varieties, often
of dubious identity, appearing – and disappearing –
with bewildering speed. In many of these the essential
gracefulness of the species has been lost in the pursuit
of new colours. The available colours range widely,
excluding only red and orange. Wild irises are found in
a wide range of habitats: moisture-loving species such
as *I. sibirica* or the European *I. pseudacorus*; those
flourishing in dry shade such as the valuable American
Pacific Coast irises (hybrids of *I. douglasiana* and other
species); and those relishing dry conditions such as the
North African *I. unguicularis* (formerly *I. stylosa*).
Many of these, and their garden varieties, provide

marvellous, easy garden plants, quite undemanding as to cultivation. Some of the most exquisite are often too small, or too demanding, to make adaptable garden plants. But many of them – such as *I. reticulata*, *I. bucharica* or *I. graebneriana* – make admirable plants for the pot or trough where they may be given exactly the conditions they need. Owners of small gardens, or those unable to tackle hard garden jobs, might well consider making a little collection of these; their cultivation is an absorbing subject and few plants can equal them for beauty. I have concentrated below on the garden-worthy species or those cultivars close in spirit to them.

Illustration: *Iris chrysographes* var. *rubella*

Iris chrysographes
Origin: Burma, China
Z: 7

❧ The distinctive quality of this iris is the exceptionally elegant form of the flowers which appear in June. The rich purple petals are long and narrow, and the falls bend sharply downwards to display a lively pattern of dark stripes on a yellow background. The upper petals curve upwards and the whole flower resembles a decorative and friendly insect. The flower stems rise to 24in/60cm and the upright leaves are almost as tall. It is best in moist soil in dappled shade in association with such things as Asiatic primulas and meconopsis (although it does not demand acid soil). *I. chrysographes* var. *rubella* (also known as *I. chrysographes* 'Rubra') is a particularly fine red-purple variety. Two outstanding cultivars have exceptionally dark, almost black, flowers: *I. chrysographes* 'Inshriach' and *I. chrysographes* 'Black Form'. All share the same handsome leaf and will form a statuesque clump of great structural presence.

Iris douglasiana
Origin: California, Oregon
Z: 7

❧ The tribe of Pacific Coast irises has produced some splendidly decorative garden cultivars hybridising with other species such as *I. bracteata*, *I. innominata*, *I. munzii* and *I. tenax*. *I. douglasiana* has bold, sword-like leaves up to 30in/75cm long. The flowers are variable in colour but most have a darker or paler violet colour with darker veins and a yellow mark in the centre of the petals – but there is also a striking creamy-white form. The cultivars have produced some

143

excellent colours including marvellous yellows such as 'Quintana'. Most of the Pacific Coast irises are found in acid sites at the edge of woodland. *I. douglasiana*, however, will tolerate alkaline soil and in my own garden, which is neutral, it flourishes. It has the additional advantage that it will flower well in shade; I have it growing under the evergreen *Photinia × fraseri* where it sparkles in the penumbra. It starts to flower quite early in April and continues producing flowers well into May. The rhizomes may be divided and replanted in enriched soil in early autumn.

Iris ensata
Origin: China, Japan
Z: 7

❧ Formerly known as *I. kaempferi*, the Japanese water-iris has in recent years given rise to a bewildering series of cultivars. The species, which flowers in June, has rich purple flowers carried on stems up to 36in/90cm tall. The buds before they open are almost black and the petals are etched with darker veins. It is a strikingly handsome flower. It needs very moist soil, at the margin of a stream or pool or planted in the shallows. It is at its best in part shade. Apart from the fairly straightforward white cultivar, *I. ensata* 'Alba', I do not know what to make of the frilly, pastel, parti-coloured, spotted, top-heavy cultivars with names like 'Prairie Love Song' or 'Moonlight Waves'. There are about 100 cultivars available commercially in Britain but only a handful are sold by more than one nursery. I cannot believe they will win the hearts of many gardeners in Britain.

Iris 'Katharine Hodgkin'
Origin: Garden
Z: 5

This cultivar was bred in the 1960s and has proved a much admired plant. It arose as a hybrid of *I. histrioides* and *I. winogradowii*. The flowers in March, of extraordinary delicacy, are an exquisite mixture of pale and deeper violet and rich yellow. 'Frank Elder' is similar in all respects but without the deeper shade of purple. Although they are quite tough in cultivation I think the best place for these treasures is alone in a trough or in some corner of the garden where their virtues may be appreciated in solitary splendour. They are very easily propagated by potting up the so-called 'rice-grain' bulbils which form at the base.

Illustration:
Iris laevigata 'Alba'

Iris laevigata
Origin: Asia
Z: 7

In its native habitat this iris is a plant of the waterlogged banks of streams and pools. It may even grow with its roots in the water. It will grow to 24in/60cm high and it flowers in June. The violet petals spread widely creating a graceful winged shape which is emphasised by the slender stripes of yellow which run down the centre of each petal. It must have, at the very least, moisture-retentive soil and it will flower well in full sun or part shade. There are many good cultivars of which the white variety, *I. laevigata* 'Alba' is especially fine, with violet stripes on the inner petals. *I. laevigata* is a refined plant and I have seen it well used in an underwater container in a formal stone-edged pool. It may be propagated by division in early autumn.

Iris latifolia
Origin: Spain
Z: 7

❧ Formerly known as *I. xiphioides*, this was most confusingly referred to as 'the English iris.' In its native habitat in the Spanish Pyrenees it is a plant of damp meadows. The flowers, which open in June, are a splendid rich violet-blue with petals of silky texture and falls marked with white and yellow. It grows up to 24in/60cm tall and the stems and leaves are a striking pale green with a hint of blue in it which makes a striking complement to the flowers. This is an iris which is suitable, as in nature, for naturalising in a meadow garden. It needs damp soil and an open sunny position. There is a good white form, *I. latifolia alba*, and a deeply disappointing pale violet form but neither has the *éclat* of the original.

Iris magnifica
Origin: Central Asia
Z: 5

❧ This is one of the Juno irises, all of which come from Central and Western Asia. It is, as the name says, a magnificent plant, one of the larger irises, with stems rising as high as 36in/90cm. Apart from the beauty of the flowers its great ornamental attraction is its statuesque form. From its thick fleshy stems handsome leaves stick out slightly upwards and in from their bases the flowering stems appear in late April or May. The flowers are white, of a silken texture with undulating edges. The falls of the petals are marked with yellow and in many plants there is a vague hint of blue towards the base of the petals. This is an easy garden plant, doing well in rich soil but demanding a sunny position. In its season few other herbaceous plants can compare for its dazzling impact. In the wild it is found in remote, dry mountainous places – as high as 5,000ft/1,500m – in the winter the rhizomes are buried deep under snow. In the garden it will prove a trouble-free plant, looking marvellous among the new foliage of astrantias, euphorbias and geraniums.

Iris missouriensis
Origin: W. United States
Z: 6

❦ It is the combination of foliage and flowers that makes the Missouri flag one of the finest species irises. The leaves are upright, quite narrow, blade-like, a very decorative pale glaucous grey. The flowers in May, carried on 24in/60cm stems, are pale lavender-blue, elegantly formed with narrow petals. The falls are veined with blue markings, as though painted with a fine brush, and marked with lemon yellow in the throat. In the wild it is found in alkaline soil and in the garden it should have a sunny position. In flower it is a dazzling sight – and the strongly architectural foliage continues to give pleasure long after flowering. There is a pretty white cultivar, *I. missouriensis* 'Alba'. *I. longipetala*, from the same area, is very similar.

Iris orientalis
Origin: Greece, Turkey
Z: 8

❦ Few irises can touch this for beauty and presence. In favourable conditions it will form a clump up to 5ft/1.5m tall with the flowers rising slightly above the tips of the leaves. The leaves are stiff, erect and blade-like, slightly glaucous in colour and looking marvellous with light shining through them. The flowers in June are white, with well-separated petals

which have decoratively crimped edges and whose centres are suffused with pale yellow. The falls arch downwards gracefully, and the other petals strain upwards. The flowers have a sweet, persistent scent. It is the mixture of boldness and delicacy that makes this an exceptional iris. In the wild it is a plant of wet places, often found in salt-marshes. In the garden it will need at the very least rich, moisture-retentive soil where it will soon form a statuesque clump. It will flower well in sun or part-shade and would be marvellous on the banks of a pool or stream under the light canopy of a tree.

Iris pallida
Origin: S.E. Europe
Z: 5

❧ The Dalmatian iris is one of the finest of the larger bearded irises. The large flowers in May are a beautiful clear lavender-blue with undulating petals intricately marked with darker veins. The beards are creamy white tipped with yellow. Flowering stems will rise to over 36in/90cm with as many as six flowers on each one. The leaves are a good pale glaucous green, quite short in relation to the flower stems, no more than 24in/60cm. There is an excellent variegated cultivar, *I. pallida* 'Variegata', whose leaves are broadly striped with creamy yellow along their length. This is a magnificent border iris. It is a large and characterful plant and any associated planting needs to be in scale; I have seen it looking marvellous with *Euphorbia characias* ssp. *wulfenii* 'Lambrook Gold' which has large pale lime-green flower head. Many hybrid cultivars among large bearded irises are derived from *I. pallida*, few rival it for beauty.

Iris pseudacorus
Origin: Europe
Z: 5

❧ The yellow flag, growing on the banks of streams and lakes, is a plant of bold character. It is an essential plant for any garden that has natural water. It has a statuesque form with stiffly upright blade-like leaves up to 4ft/1.2m high. They are glaucous in colour with finely shaded stripes running along their length. The flowers in May are a fine lemon yellow and their falls are marked with an etching of fine dark grey lines like a piece of Rococo embroidery. Several flowers are carried on each stem some of which are partly hidden among the foliage. There is a cultivar with handsomely variegated leaves, *I. pseudacorus* 'Variegata' with an

151

especially good glaucous-grey colouring edged with silver. *I. pseudacorus* will form an emphatic clump that is quite able to hold its own with even the larger waterside plants like *Gunnera manicata*. It does not depend upon a waterside site – it will grow quite well in heavy, moisture-retentive soil. However, it looks its best in a naturalistic setting.

Illustration:
Iris sanguinea 'Alba'

Iris sanguinea
Origin: Japan, Korea, Russia
Z: 5

This beautiful iris has much in common with *I. sibirica* but with a character all of its own. Mature clumps form striking sheaves of stiff, upright blade-like leaves which will rise as high as 36in/90cm having emphatic architectural presence. The flowers in late May or June are carried at the tips of slender stems and the flowers themselves are elegantly formed with narrow petals, the falls curving widely. They are rich purple in colour and the falls are marked with tiger stripes in yellow-brown. It is best in damp, rich soil and will flower very well in part shade. It is a marvellous woodland plant in a naturalistic setting, on the edge of a glade or stream. There is an exquisite white cultivar, *I. sanguinea* 'Alba'.

Iris sibirica
Origin: Europe, Russia,
Turkey
Z: 4

❧ The Siberian iris is a versatile plant – one of the easiest and most valuable of its tribe. The flowers, carried at the tips of very thin stems, appear in May. They are neatly formed, with narrow petals, an excellent rich purple-blue. The throats of the falls are intricately marked with a fretwork of dark purple, pale yellow and flecks of red-brown – exactly the same markings are to be seen on the outside of the buds before they open. The leaves are narrow, upright and slightly curving, rising 24in/60cm, almost as high as the flowers – they form a graceful sheaf. I grow it in several places in the garden and have found that it does equally well in sun or in part-shade. It prefers rich, heavy soil. I have seen it used as a lovely underplanting to the tree mallow *Abutilon* × *suntense* which has silver-lilac flowers which appear at the same time as the iris. It has been crossed with *I. sanguinea* to produce good cultivars. 'Heavenly Blue' has much of the upright *Sibirica* character with soft pale blue flowers. Among white-flowered cultivars 'White Queen' and 'White Swirl' are very attractive.

Illustration: *Iris unguicularis* 'Walter Butt'

Iris unguicularis
Origin: North Africa
Z: 8

This, formerly known as *I. stylosa*, is one of the truly essential garden plants. The flowers are of marvellous beauty but the fact that they appear in winter, when nothing remotely as lovely is to be seen, is their trump card. The leaves give no hint of the beauties to come – they are grass-like, rather coarse, 24in/60cm long and some dead leaves are always apparent. The emergence of the flowers – at any time from late autumn to February – is one of the most exciting moments in the garden. Pale green fleshy stems, no more than 12in/30cm tall, unfurl revealing pale violet flowers. The petals curl back to show an interior striped with white and violet and marked with a smudge of lemon. The flowers are sweetly scented – all

Illustration: *Iris unguicularis* 'Mary Barnard'

the more noticeable if you bring them indoors and display them in a vase. It must have a sunny, well protected site and many gardeners say that it does best in poor, stony soil. But in my own garden, with its rich clay, it seems to flourish. I have it growing at the foot of a bush of rosemary. The white form, *I. unguicularis alba*, with the same lemon yellow markings is if anything more beautiful. Particularly good cultivars are *I. unguicularis* 'Walter Butt' with much paler colouring, an almost silver violet; *I unguicularis* 'Mary Barnard' with sparkling blue-purple flowers; and *I. unguicularis* 'Bob Thompson' with a rich purple colour. Many authorities say that *I. unguicularis* resents disturbance. I divided a plant of the white form in the late spring and it flowered beautifully the following winter. The one certain thing is that it will flower best if it has had a good baking in the summer.

Ixiolirion

Ixiolirion tataricum
Origin: Asia
Z: 7

There are four species of ixiolirion in the family Amaryllidaceae/Liliaceae.

ɤ This is a very beautiful summer-flowering bulb that needs hot, dry conditions to flower at its best. Its flowers in June or July are an intense violet-blue gathered together into loose sprays. The petals are very narrow, well separated and curve backwards. The leaves are thin, rather lax, glaucous green. It will grow to a height of about 12in/30cm. It is an excellent bulb to plant with low shrubs of Mediterranean character – artemisia, cistus and sage – which enjoy the same conditions and through which the ixiolirion may grow. *Ixiolirion tataricum* Ledebourii Group (syn. *I. ledebourii*) is similar but with more vivid violet flowers.

Kniphofia

Kniphofia caulescens
Origin: South Africa
Z: 7

Illustration opposite:
Kniphofia 'Royal Standard'

There are over 60 species of kniphofia, or red hot pokers, in the family Asphodelaceae/Liliaceae. They are all rhizomatous perennials and all native to the African continent. Most of those seen in gardens are cultivars of hybrids of impenetrably complicated origins. There are some very attractive plants among these, varying from the flamboyant 'Royal Standard' which will shoot up to 4ft/1.2m flaunting its vermilion and lemon flower heads, to the demure 'Snow Maiden', 24in/60cm tall, with white flowers. There are several excellent yellow cultivars. 'Sunningdale Yellow', 24in/60cm high, which produces good soft yellow flowers over a very long period, starting as early as late May – is a marvellous border plant. 'Percy's Pride' is a little taller in a sharper shade of yellow verging on lime green. Kniphofias may be propagated by dividing clumps in late autumn or in the spring.

ɤ The flowers of this poker open in late summer, a refined salmon-pink which fades to soft cream. The flower-heads are broad at the base, narrowing towards the tip like a well-licked lollipop. The flowering stems are quite thick, rising to 4ft/1.2m and the foliage is a very decorative glaucous grey. It is marvellous rising

among pink phlox and *Tricyrtis formosana* which flower at the same time. It is among the hardiest of the pokers and is naturalised in certain parts of the east coast of Scotland.

Kniphofia sparsa
Origin: South Africa
Z: 8

❧ The naming of this poker is uncertain – it may be a synonym for *K. gracilis*. It is one of the smaller species, no more than 30in/75cm tall, with exceptionally pretty flowers which open in August. These are pink-brown – exactly the colour of the gills of a fresh field mushroom – fading to ivory at the base. As the individual flowers fade long white stamens and orange anthers are thrust out giving the lower part of the flower head a whiskery appearance. The whole flower head is very narrow, becoming pointed at the tip. The leaves curve about elegantly at the foot of the flower stems. It would make a beautiful plant for a pot and its cool elegance of form and colour will make a striking contribution to the late-summer border.

Kniphofia thomsonii var.
snowdenii
Origin: Central Africa
Z: 8

❧ This tender kniphofia is quite unlike others I describe here. It does not produce the usual bottle-brush inflorescence but instead its flowers hang outwards well spaced out along the stem which rises to a height of 36in/90cm. The flowers, which appear in July or August, are coral-pink, tubular and curve downwards resembling exotic miniature fruit. The leaves are grass-like, forming a sheaf about the base of the flowering stems. It needs a sunny position and in less favoured places a thick mulch will help to protect it in the winter. It may also be grown very successfully as a pot plant. I have seen it looking marvellous in a large urn with, at its base, the trailing *Convolvulus sabatius* with silver-blue flowers.

Kniphofia triangularis
Origin: South Africa
Z: 6

❧ The naming of this poker is a puzzle and it almost certainly covers more than one species. It is also known as *K. galpinii*. It has distinguished scarlet flowers with undertones of rust-orange carried on brown-tinged stems which rise to 36in/90cm. The flower heads are more elegant than other species with the individual flowers separated and showing their tubular shape. They open in late July or August and continue for a long period. The leaves are very thin, like grass. It gives admirable colour to the border.

Kniphofia uvaria 'Nobilis'
Origin: Garden
Z: 6

❧ This great poker is one of the most dramatic of all. Its flowering stems will rise to 6ft/1.8m bearing at their tips bold bottle-brushes of flowers a rich tomato red. The leaves are handsome, deep green, strap-like. It starts to flower in August but will continue more or less fortissimo well into autumn. Apart from the invigorating colour the larger kniphofias such as this have tremendous architectural presence, soaring above practically all other herbaceous planting. It is a superb ingredient for a richly coloured border. I have seen it marvellously used in front of a large bush of *Cotinus coggygria* 'Royal Purple' with the bold pleated leaves and scarlet flowers of *Crocosmia* 'Lucifer' at its feet.

Leucojum

Illustration opposite:
Leucojum vernum
'Gravetye Giant'

Authorities debate the meaning of the word leucojum; in Greek *leukos* means white but the second part of the word either means 'eye' or 'violet' (from the supposed scent) – neither of which is convincing. There are about ten species, all bulbous, in the family Amaryllidaceae/Liliaceae, native to North Africa, Europe and the Middle East.

Leucojum aestivum
Origin: Europe
Z: 4

❧ The word *aestivum* means summer – misleading, because *L. aestivum* flowers in the spring. The snowflake is a showier version of the snowdrop, but with a character all of its own. It forms a generous clump with soaring blade-like leaves, a lustrous rich

green, which rise to 24in/60cm. The flowers appear in April, gathered in rows at the tips of stems which rise higher than the leaves. They hang like little white bells, with scalloped tips to the petals which are tipped with green. The cultivar *L. aestivum* 'Gravetye Giant' is much superior to the type, with a bolder presence. Its flowers are larger in relation to the leaves (which in the type are often so crowded as to obscure the flowers) and as many as five flowers are carried on each stem. It is at its best in a semi-shaded position in moist soil where it makes an admirable companion with some of the paler, more delicately formed, daffodils such as 'Thalia'. It makes a good plant for the woodland garden, with quite enough presence to embellish the foot of a flowering shrub or small tree. The bulbs should be planted fairly deep – no less than 5in/13cm. Propagate by dividing clumps after flowering.

Illustration: *Leucojum vernum* 'Carpaticum'

Leucojum vernum
Origin: Europe
Z: 5

❧ The spring snowflake flowers very early, usually in February. It is a handsome plant with particularly attractive broad fresh green leaves, appearing well before the flowers, which arch gracefully, with the flower stems rising a little higher to 8in/20cm. The flowers hang downwards, white with smudges of green at the tips of the petals, resembling slightly squashed miniature lampshades. In the wild it is a plant of moist woodland and the dappled shade of hedgerows. In the garden, use it in more informal places – with ferns and hellebores, for example. The form *L. vernum* var. *carpathicum* has pretty yellow tips to the petals.

Libertia

There are about 20 species of libertia, all rhizomes, in the family Iridaceae native to South America and Australia.

Libertia formosa
Origin: Chile
Z: 8

❧ This handsome Chilean plant has a powerful architectural shape with upright blade-like evergreen foliage which rises to a height off 36in/90cm. The flowers, which appear from late May onwards, are arranged in generous, billowing upright umbels rising high above the foliage. Each flower has three rounded petals with white stamens and pale yellow anthers. The unopened flower buds are sheathed in bronze-brown making a striking contrast with the white of the opened flowers. It needs protection from the wind, is best in a sunny position and must have neutral to acid soil.

Illustration: *Lilium* 'Lady
Bowes Lyon'

Lilium

There are about 100 species of lily, in the family
Liliaceae/Liliaceae, among which are some of the
most deservedly popular of garden plants. It is hard to
imagine a garden without lilies. They are among the
most spectacularly beautiful, and marvellously scented,
of all hardy plants. Some have the reputation of being
difficult or, like tulips, of flowering once only and
gradually fading away. However, in certain conditions,
there are many lilies that will settle down, reproduce
and flower year in year out without the slightest
difficulty. In my own garden, for example, I have two
groups of the lovely panther lily, *Lilium pardalinum*,
which is entirely self-supporting, producing its
exquisite flowers without fail in early July. Even if it is
impossible to provide suitable conditions for lilies in
your garden beds, many may be grown most
successfully in pots. Most lilies flower best in
moisture-retentive soil that is neither too rich nor
excessively acidic. For these reasons manure is not
suitable and nor is bog peat. The best medium is natural

Illustration:
Lilium 'Enchantment'

leaf-mould. In the garden lily bulbs should be planted
in a shady or part-shaded position and the soil should
be enriched with leaf-mould. The perfect soil for the
largest range of lilies is one that is slightly on the acid
side of neutral. Slugs relish the bulbs and a handful or
two of sharp sand surrounding each bulb will help to
protect them. They should usually be planted 6in/15cm
deep in late winter or early spring. This is no plant for
miserly planting – bold clumps or drifts are best,
naturalistically disposed. Once established, bulbs
should not be disturbed, so be careful when digging
nearby. Many lilies are surprisingly easy and quick to
grow from seed, but some are very slow. *Lilium regale*,
for example, often produces vast quantities of seed
which, if sown in the spring, will have made a bulb by
the end of the year and produce a flower the following
summer. It is best, in fact, to remove this youthful
flower so that energy is concentrated on forming a
substantial bulb. If you sow seed every year you will
soon establish a constant supply of flowering bulbs.
The other technique for propagating lily bulbs is
scaling, in which outer layers are removed from a
mature bulb and placed in compost. The following year
they will have formed bulbils at the base which will
grow into mature, flowering bulbs. If you buy bulbs,
by far the best, and cheapest, source is a reliable

Illustration opposite:
Lilium 'Stargazer'

wholesaler who specialises in them from whom you may order by the hundred and share them out with your friends. Non-specialist sources, particularly supermarkets, too often have badly stored and relatively expensive specimens.

The International Lily Register has divided lilies into 17 categories according to their genetic derivation or their general appearance ('flat star shaped flowers' and so forth). At any one time there are at least 200 cultivars commercially available but they come and go with bewildering speed and only a few are widely available over a long period of time (such as the purple spotted heavily scented 'Star Gazer'). Some really fine lily cultivars have a very short commercial life. The splendid orange-red 'Lady Bowes Lyon' was listed in the 1994/95 *The Plant Finder* as available from one source only. In the 1995/96 edition it is no longer available. The solution for the gardener is, if you want a particular colour or style of cultivar, scrutinise the suppliers' lists and order immediately. It is futile in a book, however, to recommend cultivars that quickly become unobtainable. There are countless hybrids, sometimes of wildly improbable form and colour. These may meet the need for a very specific colour for a certain effect but few are really good garden plants. The species described below will only become unavailable if they become extinct.

Lilium auratum
Origin: Japan
Z: 6

❧ This spectacular lily is one of the species that make one wonder why the breeders bother to hybridise new varieties. It is magnificently exotic, with the largest flowers of any lily. They appear in June, flaring wide open with petals well separated and curling back at the tips, as much as 10in/25cm across. The petals are white with smudges of yellow down the centre and a scattering of deep red freckles. The anthers are very striking, orange-brown, curved, thrust out at the tips of very long stamens. Lastly, the flowers suffuse the air with a deep, rich, languorous scent. It makes a big plant, as tall as 6ft/1.8m, that will certainly need

staking. In its native Japan it grows in volcanic ash and will not thrive on rich nourishment. Try and give it a warm place, with a certain amount of shade, with the best drainage possible in rather thin acid soil. It is wonderful in a very large container where you can give it the perfect conditions.

Lilium candidum
Origin: Greece
Z: 6

❧ The Madonna lily is a breathtaking sight in full flower in June or July. The flowering stems rise to 5ft/1.5m bearing up to six dazzling white trumpet flowers, up to 5in/12cm long, with orange-yellow anthers which emphasise the flowers' whiteness. The petals are slightly furrowed and the flowers give off a delicious fresh sweet scent. This, one of the oldest garden plants in the world, is famous for flourishing in neglected corners of cottage gardens and resisting the laborious attempts of gardeners to provide the conditions that will allow it to thrive. It is susceptible to viral disease and in cottage gardens it may be the only lily present and thus not exposed to alien infections. In the wild it grows in rocky, very dry places. The solution in the garden may be to plant it in a sunny, well-drained corner, far from other lilies. Unlike other lilies the bulbs should be planted quite shallowly, with the top of the bulb breaking the surface. Most Madonna lilies available are sterile, so the usual means of propagation is bulb scaling.

Lilium chalcedonicum
Origin: Greece
Z: 5

❧ The scarlet turk's cap lily is one of the earliest European lilies to have been used as a garden plant: it was known in the 17th century and a double form, now extinct, was seen in 18th-century gardens. It grows up to 5ft/1.5m high and produces its gleaming vermilion flowers with sharply reflexed petals in June. Each stem may carry as many as ten flowers. It is susceptible to viral infections but if planted in full sun and sharply drained soil, like *L. candidum* which comes from the same sort of habitat, it will do well. It is one of the finest of the red lilies and would make a superlative ingredient in a 'hot' coloured border. There is a very attractive old garden hybrid with *L. candidum, L. × testaceum,* with ivory petals and rich orange anthers.

Lilium longiflorum
Origin: Japan, Taiwan
Z: 8

❧ This superlative lily is scarcely reliably hardy, tending to succumb to cold, wet winter weather. However, it is among the easiest and quickest to raise from seed and, in pots, it makes a marvellous ornament for terrace or conservatory. It grows to about 36in/90cm producing its fabulous trumpet-shaped flowers in June. Before they open the buds are long, very pale green, full of exciting promise. The flowers are white, still with a hint of green, with the tips of the petals curving back only slightly. There is a dab of yellow in the throat, the anthers are tawny brown and the stigma lolls in the throat like a curiously shaped tongue. They give a deep, sweetly exotic scent which evokes hot tropical nights. They are the lilies most frequently seen in expensive flower shops and street markets and known as 'longies'. For the gardener its most precious use will be as a container plant that is exceptional in all respects.

Lilium martagon
Origin: Caucasus,
Europe, Siberia
Z: 4

❧ The martagon lily is very variable and although some flower colours are more beautiful than others its stately presence and the way its flowers are carried is never less than beautiful. The flowering stems are up to 6ft/1.8m high with fresh green leaves borne in decorative whorls at regular intervals. The flowers are grouped in a loose raceme at the upper part, with as

Illustration: *Lilium
martagon* var. *album*

many as 40 flowers on each plant. The petals curve
backwards very sharply with the anthers thrown
outwards prominently, varying in colour from
egg-yolk yellow to orange-yellow. The stems bearing
each flower are horizontal with the flower carried at
the very tip hanging downwards like a miniature
lantern. In the wild it is usually found on alkaline soil
in woodland or scrub – as high as 8,000ft/2,400m. In
the garden it is one of the supreme woodland bulbs,
growing well in shade. Well-drained rich leaf mould
provides the perfect growing medium. To my eye it
never looks quite at home in a border, a wilder setting
seems much more appropriate. It varies in colour from
a rather wishy-washy pink-purple to a much finer rich
plum colour, and all have petals mottled with darker
spots. The white form *L. martagon* var. *album* is very
beautiful, as is the rich maroon *L. martagon* var.
cattaniae, neither of which has spotted flowers.
Propagation by seed or bulb scales is slow to produce
flowering bulbs but once established in an appropriate
site a community will flourish for years.

Lilium monadelphum
Origin: Caucasus
Z: 5

From the upland meadows of the Caucasus, found
as high as 8,000ft/2,400m, this great lily is one of the
finest yellow-flowered kinds. It grows to a height of
about 5ft/1.4m, with rather stiff well-leafed stems, and
its flowers open in June. As many as 20 are held on
each stem, pale lemon yellow, with petals curving

sharply backwards. The unopened buds, hanging downwards, look like very exotic bananas, tipped top and bottom with a splash of gleaming crimson, still clearly visible in the fully open flower. A good clump in full flower is one of the most marvellous sights. In the garden it will grow well in semi-shade or full sun – I have seen it spectacularly naturalised on the edge of beech woods. It will flourish in different soils, heavy or light, acid or alkaline, but it must not be waterlogged. It may be propagated by seed or by bulb scales but bulbs take a long time to reach flowering size – up to five years. Once established they will settle down and flower without trouble for a very long time.

Lilium pardalinum
Origin: W. North America
Z: 5

❧ This is the lily for those who complain how difficult it is to establish lilies in the garden. I have two large communities of it, in rather different parts of the garden, one in full sun and the other in dappled shade. They flower every year with the greatest of ease – and what flowers! They open in July, the petals curving back upon themselves to make almost spherical shapes. The petals are tipped with orange-red but the bases are a warm yellow, splashed with spots of red-brown. The stamens are thrust well out below, tipped with orange-brown anthers held on the most delicate hinges, allowing them to flutter in the slightest breeze. The flowering stems rise 6ft/1.8m high, with several flowers carried at the top. The stems are ornamented with ruffs of leaves at regular intervals. They are quite stiff and, unlike other tall lilies, need little support except perhaps neighbouring plants to nudge against. It is easily propagated by dividing the rhizomatous bulbs which quickly form substantial clumps. In the garden it will do best in rich soil. I grow it rising above the daylily *Hemerocallis fulva* but it is also spectacular as an ingredient of a border of hot reds and purples. *L. pardalinum* var. *giganteum* is a form that will grow as tall as 8ft/2.5m with an even greater profusion of flowers, as many as 30 on a stem. The same plant is also known as *L. pardalinum* 'Red Sunset'.

Lilium pumilum
Origin: China, Korea,
Mongolia, Siberia
Z: 5

❧ Among the best and easiest of the smaller-flowered lilies, *L. pumilum* has flowers of a dazzling colour. They are produced in late May or June, a lustrous vermilion with a gleaming surface. When fully open the petals curve right back upon themselves and orange stamens are thrust out. They have a curious smell, like chocolate. The flowering stems, which rise to about 24in/60cm high, are thin and wiry bearing flowers on slender side stems. In the wild it grows in quite open, exposed places but in the garden it will flower well in part shade where its gleaming, jewel-like flowers are displayed to great advantage. It is beautiful in a container. It produces huge quantities of seed but if you allow it to do so the bulbs will be deprived of nourishment. However, it is very easy to propagate by seed which will produce flowering plants within a year of sowing.

Lilium regale
Origin: China
Z: 5

❧ Despite all the hybridising of lilies, which has certainly produced some splendid colours, few lilies give such dependable pleasure as this marvellous Chinese species, introduced to the west by the great plant hunter E.H. Wilson in 1905. It flowers in June, producing white trumpets, up to 6in/15cm long, flushed with purple without and pale yellow within. The petals curve back gracefully at the tips and the flowers have a fabulous scent, sweet, spicy and intense.

A large bulb, growing vigorously in rich soil, will produce as many as 30 flowers on a single stem. It will flourish equally well in sun or in light shade and will tolerate an alkaline soil. It is one of the finest border plants and excellent in pots, suffusing a sitting area with its exquisite scent. It would come very high on many gardeners' lists of the absolutely essential plants. It may be propagated from seed sown in spring. Seedlings will produce flowers remarkably quickly, often in the second year after sowing, but these should be removed before any seed is set in order to concentrate all energy in the growth of the bulb.

Lilium speciosum var.
album
Origin: Japan
Z: 6

❧ In all respects this is one of the most beautiful of the species lilies. It flowers in August, later than others, unfurling its wide open, almost flat, white trumpets and filling the air with its intense sweet fragrance. The backs of the petals are smudged with brown-pink and their edges undulate attractively. The long anthers are deep yellow. In full flower it gives the impression of prodigal abundance. It is rather prone to viral infections and, like *L. candidum* may be best grown on its own. It needs full sun and rich, deep soil. Once established it makes a wonderful border plant, rising to about 4ft/1.2m, but tending to flop with the great weight of flowers and needing support. It may be propagated by seed. There are several cultivars and the species itself varies, with more or less crimson flushing the petals. *L. speciosum* var. *roseum* is a fine pale pink and *L. speciosum* var. *rubrum* is carmine red.

Liriope

Liriope muscari
Origin: China, Japan
Z: 6

There are about five species if liriope in the family Convallariaceae/Liliaceae.

❧ This autumn-flowering plant is valuable both for its striking flowers and ornamental foliage. The purple flowers which open in September or October are clustered together in upright spikes borne on a fleshy stem which rises to 12in/30cm. The leaves are blade-like and pointed, with a distinguished lustrous surface, and rise rather higher than the flowers. It must have a sunny position and rich, well-drained soil. It looks very beautiful with other bulbous plants which flower in the same period such as *Nerine bowdenii*. It may be propagated by dividing the rhizomes in the spring. There are several cultivars: *L. muscari* 'Monroe White' is pure white (also known as *L. muscari alba*) and *L. muscari* 'Gold-band' has gold variegated foliage.

Moraea

Moraea huttonii
Origin: South Africa
Z: 8

There are over 100 species of moraea, in the family Iridaceae, found only in southern Africa. The species described here is one of the very few hardy in European gardens.

❧ This stately iris-like plant throws out bold flowering stems, 36in/90cm long, rather fleshy with flower buds sprouting alternately along the stem. The flowers which appear in May are a fine clear yellow with intricate dark grey markings on the petals which are well separated, giving them great elegance. They give off a sweet scent, light but quite distinct. The leaves are floppy but distinguished, each one up to 4ft/1.2m long and marked with dark veins along its whole length. The foliage forms a lovely mound from

which the flower stems emerge. This will need a very sunny position in light, well-drained soil. A large clump of it is a spectacular sight. It may be propagated by dividing the corms in the autumn.

Muscari

Muscari armeniacum
Origin: Mediterranean
Z: 6

There are about 30 species, all bulbs, in the family Hyacinthaceae/Liliaceae. They are all quite small, not individually imposing, but forming decorative splashes of colour, sometimes richly scented, in spring.

❧ The Armenian grape hyacinth has flowers of a wonderfully intense blue that seems to glow on even the dullest day. They are upright racemes composed of tightly-packed 'rugby-football-like bells' as the plant-hunter Reginald Farrer called them. The flowering head is up to 3in/8cm long held on a bright green stem of similar length. It is best in a sunny position and will flourish in poor soil provided it is well drained. It will make its greatest impact in the form of a bold clump – this is no plant for spotty planting. It looks especially beautifully with the pale silver grey of such plants as santolina or the slightly glaucous foliage of pinks – both of which enjoy the same conditions.

Muscari comosum
'Plumosum'
Origin: Garden
Z: 4

❧ The Mediterranean tassel hyacinth is a pretty plant, flowering in May or June, with racemes of flowers in upright spikes with the lower flowers brown/purple and the upper ones varying in colour from blue to violet and, best of all, an intense dark violet. It has the curious characteristic of some of the upper flowers being sterile and sprouting upwards at the top forming the stiff tassel that gives the plant its common name. In the form *M. comosum* 'Plumosum' *all* the flowers are sterile making the flower-head resemble a froth of flowers. The flower stem rises to 10in/25cm and as they are fairly slender they are often bent down by the weight of the flowers. It does best in full sun and is a highly decorative front-of-the-border plant.

Muscari macrocarpum
Origin: E. Mediterranean
Z: 7

❧ The flower stems rise from a mass of fleshy, glistening leaves up to 12in/30cm long. The flowers in April are borne at the tips of stems up to 6in/12.5cm long, upright racemes of diminutive tubes, like miniature uncurved bananas. Those at the top are a violet-brown colour, those at the bottom, banana yellow. The flowers give off a scent of tropical sweetness. It must have a sunny, warm position in well-drained soil – damp, heavy soil will kill it quickly. It is excellent at the front of a raised terrace, or in a rock garden, but in either case raised up so that its delicious perfume may be savoured. If your garden cannot provide the right conditions, it makes an excellent pot plant.

Illustration:
Narcissus tazetta

Narcissus

The name of the daffodil family comes from the Greek for sleepiness or torpor, because of the supposed narcotic properties of the bulbs. There are about 50 species in the family Amaryllidaceae/ Liliaceae, native to southern Europe, the Mediterranean region, China and Japan. Although there is only a small number of species the number of named cultivars is gigantic – running into several thousands. New cultivars continue to appear but there seem to be no valuable additions to the present repertory of truly valuable garden plants. However, from the gardener's point of view the choice is made easier because there are only a few distinctive types.

For ease of classification daffodils have been dvided by the International Registration Authority into 12 groups defined either by the general appearance (for example daffodils with emphatic 'trumpets' or coronas) or by their origins (for example those descended from species such as *N. tazetta* or *N. poeticus*). The species, rarely seen in gardens, are an exceptionally attractive group but some of them have such specific cultivation requirements that make it difficult to accommodate them in the mixed plantings of most gardens. Most daffodil cultivars are undemanding, flourishing in soil of different kinds provided there is enough moisture and at the very least a position which gets some sunlight.

I think that the most beautiful use for daffodils is in a naturalistic context. A spreading group of the delicate *N. cyclamineus* under a deciduous tree or shrub, or of the deliciously scented poet's narcissus (*N. poeticus*) planted in the grass of an orchard, give greater pleasure than artful arrangements in the garden. Many of the

Illustration:
Narcissus cyclamineus

garden cultivars have a coarse shape – often with excessively large flowers of a strident, brassy colour. In massed plantings in public places the detail of an individual plant is much less important than the expanse of colour. In small private gardens, however, the defects of such plants will be all too visible. The most distinguished of the species, on the other hand, are always worth looking at in detail. Some of the more delicate of them are perhaps best planted in troughs or pots where not only is it possible to provide the perfect environment but they may be admired from close up. Several of the species have wonderful scent – very

Illustration: *Narcissus* 'Eystettensis'

rarely found in the highly hybridised varieties.

Most modern cultivars are derived from the western European wild daffodil, *N. pseudonarcissus*, forms of which have been valued garden plants for hundreds of years. The double-flowered *N.* 'Eystettensis' (also known as *N.* 'Capax Plenus') has been known since the 17th century and is still available commercially. It has very double flowers of an excellent pale creamy yellow.

Daffodils may be grown successfully in pots but it is only really worthwhile for the kinds that need special treatment. The scented species such as *N. jonquilla* or *N. tazetta* which I describe in more detail below make marvellous indoor ornaments or arranged on a sunny terrace. High temperatures will often prevent them from flowering. If you are proposing to force bulbs for early flowering they should be put in a protected but cool place (no more than 55°F). When the flower buds have been formed they may be brought indoors but they will still be best in the coolest part of the house.

Illustration: *Narcissus* 'Peeping Tom'

The soil should be slightly alkaline and moisture retentive; it should have no manure or extra nitrogen. As a general rule bulbs should be planted so that the depth of earth above them is equal to one-and-a-half bulb depths.

Probably the most common site for daffodils is in long grass on the verges of paths or in an orchard or meadow garden. Bulbs should be planted 6in/10cm deep, in a sunny or partly-shaded position. The grass should not be cut until the daffodil leaves have died down – which is usually at least six weeks after they have flowered. Although I have been successful with Pheasant's Eye narcissus, *N. poeticus*, in an orchard it is often the case that the vigorous hybrids are the most reliable for this purpose. At all events, do plant them in flowing drifts, avoiding any hint of regimentation. Bulbs should be planted no later than the end of September.

I have picked out a few of the species that I find particularly attractive – I give details of them below. So far as the cultivars are concerned, my taste is for those with paler colours and graceful petals. There are well over 700 named varieties on the market, an absurd proliferation. Here I pick out some that seem to me both to be especially attractive and to do well in gardens. They are arranged in order of season of

Illustration: *Narcissus* 'Jenny'

flowering. 'February Gold', 12in/30cm high, which flowers in March rather than February, has a neat trumpet of a cheerful yellow and elegantly-formed paler petals that sweep backwards. 'February Silver' is a much paler version. Both these are derived from *N. cyclamineus*. 'Peeping Tom', also flowering in March, has a similar character but is larger, up to 18in/45cm. It has a long narrow trumpet with a crisply frilled mouth and swept back petals. Its colour is a clear rich yellow – striking and warm but without a hint of brassiness. 'Pride of Cornwall' flowers at the end of March. It is derived from *N. tazetta* and has a deep gold flattened trumpet and almost white petals. It grows up to 15in/35cm tall. 'Jenny', 10in/25cm high, has very pale petals which curve backwards and a pale yellow furrowed trumpet. It flowers in early April. 'Hawera' which flowers in early April has several small flowers, an excellent sprightly lemon yellow, which hang downwards at the tips of quite short stems, no more than 8in/15cm.

Illustration:
Narcissus bulbocodium

N. bulbocodium (Zone 6), the hoop petticoat daffodil, comes from the western Mediterranean region. The flowers which open in March have a distinctive shape, 2in/5cm long, strikingly resembling an old-fashioned full-length petticoat. They are held on short stems, 3–4in/8–10cm high, and the flowers are horizontal or droop slightly, varying in colour from pale lemon yellow to a rather richer gold. The leaves are very thin and grass-like. In the wild it grows in mountain meadows, usually on acidic soil and in the garden it is excellent for naturalising in short grass. The white hoop petticoat daffodil, *N. cantabricus*, is almost identical except with creamy white flowers and it is slightly less hardy (Zone 8).

N. cyclamineus (Zone 6), from Spain and Portugal has slender tubular flowers with the tepals swept straight back, which gives them a slight resemblance to the flowers of a cyclamen. The flowers are 2in/5cm long, warm yellow in colour, appearing in March carried on the tips of slender stems up to 9in/23cm tall, which allows them to nod in a breeze. In their native habitat they grow in damp meadows, often at the edge of a stream or pool. In the garden they naturalise well in partly shaded places under deciduous trees or shrubs, benefiting from dry conditions when dormant.

N. jonquilla (Zone 4) from Spain and Portugal has tall stems, 10in/25cm long, with several flowers held at the tip and grass-like foliage. The flowers appear in late March or April, rather flat and delicately formed, egg-yolk yellow, and giving off a marvellous rich, intense perfume. It must have a well-drained position in the sunniest part of the garden. In the wild it is found in rocky places in limestone. The recently discovered *N. cordubensis* is similar in all respects.

N. poeticus (Zone 4), the poet's, or pheasant's eye, narcissus is particularly valuable because it flowers very late – well into May – and has an exceptional rich, spicy scent. The flowers are white, with well-separated twisting petals framing a very short cupped corona which is lemon-yellow within and edged with a frilly scarlet rim. It is found in moist meadows, often in mountainous regions as high as 7,500ft/2,300m. In the garden it is marvellous planted in grass in a meadow garden or orchard, where it will naturalise easily. *N. poeticus recurvus*, sometimes known as Old Pheasant's Eye, has especially beautifully backwards sweeping petals. *N.* 'Actaea' is a Dutch cultivar with larger

Illustration:
Narcissus 'Actaea'

flowers, 3in/8cm across, and much taller stems – up to 18in/45cm tall – but with much of the beauty of the type and, best of all, the same fortissimo scent.

N. tazetta (Zone 8) is native to the Mediterranean region as far east as Iran. The flowers are carried in groups – as many as seven on one stem – at the tip of tall stems up to 18in/45cm high. Each flower is up to 1 1/2in/4cm across and the cupped corona is lemon yellow framed by cream tepals which are wavy with pointed tips. The flowers are marvellously scented, intense, sweet and spicy – a bunch in a vase will perfume a room. With its soft colouring and sprays of delicate flowers at the tips of thin stems this is one of the most elegant of the daffodils. It is among the less hardy of those mentioned here and in many gardens will need a sunny, protected place. Here, flowering in March, it will provide distinctive elegance and scent the air on a warm day. The paper-white narcissus, *N. papyraceus*, is very similar in all respects except that the flowers are pure white. It is often used as a pot plant for forcing as a marvellously scented indoor ornament at Christmas time.

N. triandrus (Zone 4) is found in Portugal, Spain and North-western France in woods and open places. It produces its flowers in April, delicately formed, varying in colour from pale creamy-yellow to white, with petals swept gracefully back from the corona. It grows no more than 4in/10cm high. In the garden it will need light soil, good drainage and a sunny position. A modern cultivar with something of the species' character, but a tougher disposition, is *N.* 'Thalia', which is much larger, up to 12in/30cm high, with white flowers and a good scent.

Nectaroscordum

This genus has been separated from Allium with which it has very close connections. There are two species of bulbs in the family Alliaceae/Liliaceae.

❧ This extremely decorative plant, formerly known as *Allium siculum*, has invasive tendencies but any keen gardener will be happy to put up with them for the beauty of the flowers. These, appearing in May and June, are gathered together in profuse umbels at the tips of stems that rise to 4ft/1.2m. Each flower is bell-shaped and hangs gracefully downwards on curving stems. There are two sub-species, *N. siculum*

ssp. *siculum* and *N. siculum* ssp. *bulgaricum* which have interbred, diluting their identity. The flowers of the former tend towards red-brown with shades of green whereas those of the latter are cream and pink. Plants deriving from these hybrids are widely found in gardens, showing varying character and colours. When the flowers fade the seed-pods point upwards, resembling rockets aimed at the sky. These seed-pods are strikingly ornamental but gardeners worried about too many offspring will remove them before they scatter their seeds. The beauty of this plant derives from its elegantly-shaped and subtly coloured flowers and its ability to rise up through densely packed plantings. The dark flowers of *N. siculum* ssp. *siculum* look wonderful with deep purple columbines, *Aquilegia vulgaris,* which flower at the same time.

Illustration:
Nerine bowdenii

Nerine

There are about 30 species of nerine, all bulbs and all native to South Africa, in the family Amaryllidaceae/Liliaceae. They are among the most beautiful of bulbous plants but virtually all the species, except *Nerine bowdenii* described below are winter flowering. However, some of the tender species are commercially available and make exquisite house plants – indeed far more beautiful than most of the plants normally thought of under that term.

Nerine bowdenii
Origin: South Africa
Z: 9

❧ As the last flowers disappear from the border, this nerine provides a wonderfully exotic flowering treat for the autumn. It flowers in September or October, the fleshy stems rising 24in/60cm crowned with a group of exquisitely formed sprightly pink trumpets. The petals have undulating margins and curve sharply backwards at the tips. They have blurred stripes of a deeper pink and purple anthers are thrust out. The foliage, appearing with the flowers, is strap-like, floppy and has a handsome glistening surface. It will remain in place until before flowering time the following year. It must be planted in a sunny place – the best groups I have seen have invariably been planted against a sunny wall. Although most authorities say that good drainage is also essential I have seen it very successfully grown in heavy clay. Bulbs should not be planted too deeply – the tips should be quite close to the surface. If groups become very congested they will not flower well and should be divided. A cultivar, *N. bowdenii* 'Mark Fenwick' (sometimes also known as *N. bowdenii* 'Fenwick's Variety'), is more floriferous and has larger flowers – by no means necessarily an improvement.

Nomocharis

There are about five species of nomocharis in the family Liliaceae/Liliaceae all native to Asia.

Nomocharis pardanthina punctulata
Origin: China
Z: 7

❧ This lily-like plant has irresistible charm. Its flowers in July are white, downward facing, generously freckled with purple spots and have a purple centre. The petals are slightly frilly and open out until the flower is almost completely flat, 3in/8cm across. The flowering stems rise as high 36in/90cm and as many as 20 flowers, hanging from horizontal stems, are borne on each stem. In the wild it enjoys high rainfall, acid soil and a generally cool climate. If you do not have such conditions it will not flourish. If you do, few bulbous plants will give more exquisite pleasure. It is, I think, very much a plant for a naturalistic setting of a woodland kind.

Ornithogalum

There are about 80 species of ornithogalum, all bulbs, in the family Hyacinthaceae/Liliaceae. They are native to Europe, Western Asia and southern Africa.

Ornithogalum arabicum
Origin: Mediterranean
Z: 9

❧ This very beautiful bulb is, alas, not very hardy but well worth trying if you can give it well-drained soil and a warm, sunny position. It flowers in May or June bearing a cluster of flowers at the tip of a fleshy stem which rises 18in/45cm high. Each flower is white, globe-shaped at first, and opens out to about 2in/5cm across revealing silky petals tipped with green, orange-yellow stamens and a striking glistening black ovary at the centre. As the plant ages the flowering stems tend to twist. In the rights conditions it will produce many bulbils providing a very easy means of propagation. *O. corymbosum* is said to be almost identical but hardier but I have never seen it listed by any nurseryman.

Ornithogalum montanum
Origin: Italy, W. Asia
Z: 6

❧ In the wild this charming little flower is found in mountainous, rocky regions, often in meadows. It is the sort of modest plant that is easy to overlook but closer inspection shows character and beauty. Its six-petalled star-shaped flowers appear in April or May. They are white and veins run the whole length of the petals giving them an elegant appearance. The backs of the petals are striped with green and unopened buds show green and white stripes. The prominent stamens are the palest yellow. It makes an attractive underplanting for ornamental shrubs and would look pretty in a meadow garden, provided the grass has been cut fairly short the previous season.

Ornithogalum nutans
Origin: Balkans
Z: 6

❧ The details of this little ornithogalum are very beautiful. The leaves are rather lax and the fleshy flower stem rises among them to a height of 12in/30cm. Up to a dozen little flowers are carried, appearing in April, hanging elegantly downwards on curved stems, each shaped like a wide trumpet with flaring petals. They are white but with grey-green stripes down the centre of the petals. The anthers are pale lemon yellow. The plant is exceptionally graceful in appearance with the flowers nodding in the slightest breeze. In the wild it grows in poor soil. In the garden it will do well in part shade but it must have good drainage. I have seen it naturalised in deciduous woodland and it is quite happy in completely dry soil in the summer. It will self seed lavishly or it may be propagated by dividing clumps of bulbs in the autumn.

Ornithogalum pyrenaicum
Origin: Europe
Z: 7

❧ This summer-flowering ornithogalum throws out tall, fleshy stems up to 36in/90cm. The flowers in June are gathered in tall racemes resembling heads of barley of exquisite elegance. Each flower has very narrow petals, pale green-gold with a green stripe down the centre. The foliage is strap-like, lax and forms a cushion at the base of the flowering stem. In the wild it is found in meadows and light woodland, as high as 4,000ft/1,200m. In the garden it is at its best in wilder places where it will bring a character of airy gracefulness. It would be superlative in a meadow garden – but you would have to leave grass-cutting very late to allow the seed to develop. I have seen a group of it grown successfully in a very large pot. Here, it should have rich moisture-retentive soil.

Oxalis

Oxalis oregana
Origin: W. North America
Z: 7

There are over 800 species of oxalis, in the family Oxalidaceae, very widely distributed.

❧ This American oxalis is a decorative plant for ground cover with the bonus of ornamental flowers. The foliage is boldly shaped, like clover with heart-shaped leaves. The flowers, which appear from late spring to mid summer vary: the best are an attractive pale pink, but they may be a rather wishy-washy mauve or white. In the wild it is a woodland plant, flourishing in moist leaf-mould. In the garden it is marvellous edging a path in a wilder part of the garden or providing a flowing pool of foliage under a shrub or tree. It will form a spreading colony and is easily propagated by division in the autumn.

Illustration:
Paradisea lusitanica

Paradisea

Paradisea liliastrum
Origin: S. Europe
Z: 7

There are only two species in this genus of rhizomatous plants belonging to the family Asphodelaceae/Liliaceae.

❧ This lovely plant is rarely seen in gardens, yet it presents no particular problems of cultivation. Fleshy stems rise to 24in/60cm with flowers grouped at the top. From waxy green-tipped buds the flowers open in June, slightly ragged trumpets with pointed petals, a

dazzling white with a glistening silken texture. The leaves are grouped together in a loose rosette about the base of the stem. It is not demanding as to soil but needs a sunny position. It is an admirable border plant, rising decoratively above lower closely-packed plants. It may be propagated by dividing the rhizomes in the autumn or, a much lengthier process, by seed. A larger-flowered cultivar, *P. liliastrum* 'Major', is occasionally seen but it lacks the delicacy of the type.

Paradisea lusitanica
Origin: Portugal, Spain
Z: 7

❧ In the right conditions this splendid plant will rise to 6ft/1.8m bearing its graceful plumes of flowers swaying elegantly on slender stems. The flower buds are gathered in a tightly-packed bunch at the tip of the stem. The flowers, which open in June, are white, star-shaped with long white stamens tipped with yellow. The foliage is inconspicuous in relation to the height of the flower stem, a ring of flaccid leaves about its base. It needs rich, moist soil and a position in full sun. Clumps of it are marvellous among shrub roses or rising among other plantings in a border. It is easy to propagate by division in autumn or by seed.

Polygonatum

T he Greek origin of the name means 'many joints', referring to the angular form of the stems. There are about 30 species, all rhizomes, in the family Convallariaceae/Liliaceae, widely distributed in North America, Asia and Europe.

Polygonatum × *hybridum*
Origin: Garden
Z: 6

❧ The most commonly seen type of Solomon's Seal, an essential garden plant, is a hybrid between two species found in Asia and Europe, *P. multiflorum* and *P. odoratum*. The sweet scent of the latter has almost entirely disappeared in its hybrid but in other respects it is superior to its parents. The emerging shoots are very beautiful, a distinguished pale grey, and looking very edible. The stems, which retain a grey-purple base with a decorative bloom, grow as tall as 36in/90cm with leaves carried alternately along much of their length. These are beautifully shaped, furrowed, pale green becoming distinctly glaucous as they age. The stems flop over, sprawling horizontally, with the flowers hanging below, up to four on each stem. They are little white tubes no more than 1in/2.5cm long, opening out slightly at the mouth and tipped with green. I grow it in complete shade with ferns, the mottled *Arum italicum* ssp. *italicum* 'Marmoratum' and the ground carpeted with the shining leaves of *Asarum europaeum*. But it will also flourish in part shade and I have seen it looking wonderful in a white border as a backdrop to the tulip 'Spring Green' whose flowers are a soft white flushed with green. Two cultivars are fairly widely seen: *P.* × *hybridum* 'Flore Pleno' has double flowers but you will have to look very closely to notice; and one with a variegated leaf, *P.* × *hybridum* 'Striatum' (also known as 'Variegatum'), seems to have lost some of the hybrid vigour and always looks rather sickly to me. A much more beautiful variegated

Solomon's Seal is *P. odoratum* var. *pluriflorum* 'Variegatum' whose leaves are most beautifully edged with cream, as though with brushstrokes by a skilful artist – a lovely effect. The flowers, furthermore, are sweetly scented. There is also a double-flowered cultivar, *P. odoratum* 'Flore Pleno', which has a blowsy charm of its own. All may be propagated by dividing clumps of rhizomes in the autumn.

Puschkinia

Puschkinia scilloides
Origin: Caucasus, Iran, Turkey
Z: 5

There is one species of puschkinia in the family Hyacinthaceae/Liliaceae.

❧ This, also known as *P. libanotica,* is a marvellous March-flowering bulb which has all the freshness of spring. Its flowers are carried on crowded spikes which rise to a height of 8in/20cm. Each flower is star-shaped, the palest blue with a crisp dark stripe down the middle of the petals. The leaves are a fresh glistening green, broad and pointed at the tip. It will flourish in almost any garden soil, in part shade as well as in full sun. In the wild the bulb dries out completely in the summer and in the garden it may enjoy similar conditions under deciduous shrubs such as magnolias or viburnums. *P. scilloides* var. *libanotica* is a form with slightly smaller flowers than the type. There is an attractive pure white cultivar of this form, *P. scilloides* var. *libanotica* 'Alba'.

Ranunculus

Ranunculus ficaria
Origin: Europe
Z: 5

The buttercup family, Ranunculaceae, contains about 400 herbaceous plants widely distributed throughout the temperate parts of the world. Most have fibrous roots but those described here are tuberous.

❧ The lesser celandine is a common European wild flower found in moist places in hedgerows, verges and deciduous woodland. The type, pretty though it may be in the wild, is too invasive for the more manicured parts of the garden. However there are several cultivars that have great garden presence. *R. ficaria* 'Brazen

Illustration: *Ranunculus
ficaria* 'Salmon's White'

Hussy' has wonderful foliage, a very dark bronze-
purple with deeply-veined heart-shaped leaves. The
flowers, 1in/2.5cm across, are carried on fleshy stems
and are a gleaming golden yellow, each flower lasting a
short time, but appearing repeatedly in March. It will
form a generous clump 4in/10cm high. *R. ficaria*
'Randall's White' has the green, marbled foliage of the
type but with striking flowers with creamy-white
petals and a bold tuft of lemon-yellow stamens. *R.
ficaria* 'Salmon's White' is similar. *R. ficaria aurantiacus*
(formerly *R. ficaria* 'Cupreus') has rich copper-
coloured flowers. The curiously named *R. ficaria*
'Double Mud' is yellow with white tips to the petals
and a dark centre. *R. ficaria flore-pleno* is a fully double
form. *R. ficaria* is naturally very variable and new
cultivars are constantly popping up. The foliage of all
celandines dies down by the end of the spring and they
may be propagated by dividing clumps.

Rhodohypoxis

There are about six species of rhodohypoxis in the family Hypoxidaceae, all perennials native to South Africa.

Rhodohypoxis baurii
Origin: South Africa
Z: 8

❧ This very decorative little tuber is often restricted to the rockery but, in the right conditions, it will make a good border plant. It is low growing, rising no more than 4in/10cm, forming a spreading cushion of narrow, hairy leaves. The flowers appear from June onwards and continue in great profusion for several weeks. They are star-shaped, with petals that overlap curiously at the centre. They range in colour from white to a rich cardinal red with some rather disappointing wishy-washy pinks and purples. In the wild they are found high in the Drakensberg mountains growing in well-drained peat. In the garden they will do best in a sunny exposure with plenty of moisture in the growing season – but none in the winter. They will not survive a winter in heavy, sodden soil. In the garden they find a decorative home at the front of a border intermingling with other plants of comparable scale which flower at the same time, such as diascias, trailing herbaceous potentillas and pinks. It is also excellent in pots – plant a single colour to the brim. It may be propagated by division. There are several cultivars of *R. baurii* and of hybrids. *R. baurii* 'Douglas' is a fine rich red and *R. baurii* 'Albrighton' is rosy red. *R. baurii* 'Margaret Rose' is a refined, pale pink. *R. baurii* 'Apple Blossom' is a very decorative mixture of green and pink.

Romulea

There are about 80 species of romulea, all corms, in the family Iridaceae and native to South Africa, Europe and the Mediterranean region. Many need protection in cooler European gardens but it is a delightful genus and would make an excellent subject to collect for the cool greenhouse.

Romulea nivalis
Origin: Lebanon
Z: 8

❧ The flowers are borne on wiry stems that rise to a height of 4in/10cm. They open in March or April, beautiful pale lilac trumpets with a vivid yellow base and dark smudging on the backs of the petals which are pointed and curl backwards gracefully. The leaves strongly resemble those of crocus – narrow, upright and pointed with a pale stripe running their length, rising rather higher than the flowers. In the wild it is found as high as 7,000ft/2,000m in places which are bone dry in summer. In the garden it should have gritty, well-drained soil in a sunny position.

Roscoea

There are about 15 species of roscoea in the ginger family, Zingiberaceae.

Roscoea auriculata
Origin: Himalaya
Z: 6

❧ Many people on first seeing this lovely plant assume it to be an orchid. It stirs into life and flowers late in the season, from August to September, bringing a note of spring-like freshness to the garden. The flowers are rich purple with petals like rather floppy wings, several flowers emerging one after the other, as a magician draws streamers from his hand. The flowering stems are up to 18in/45cm high, pale green and fleshy, with handsome broad shining leaves emerging horizontally. It will flower well in sun or in part shade and needs well-drained acid loam. It is a graceful and delicate plant, perhaps at its best in a little corner of its own.

Roscoea cautleoides
Origin: Himalayas
Z: 6

This beautiful plant looks at first sight like a slightly lopsided iris to which it is not even vaguely related. It flowers in June, unfurling the palest yellow petals which glisten like fine silk. Some petals flop downwards and have ruffled edges. The fleshy stems will grow to a height of 18in/45cm with attractive fresh green undulating leaves emerging horizontally up the stem. It is at its best in deep, rich acid soil with good drainage and need at least part shade. It may be propagated by dividing the rhizomes in early spring, or by seed. Many gardeners report self-sown seedlings. This is a lovely plant to follow after erythroniums, hellebores and snowdrops as it enjoys the same conditions. The rhizomes should be planted quite deep, with 6in/15cm of soil above their crowns.

Sanguinaria

The bloodroot, in the family Papaveraceae, has a single species. It is a rhizome whose name derives from its red sap.

Sanguinaria canadensis
Origin: E. N. America
Z: 4

The bloodroot is one of the most mysterious and beautiful of plants. Its shoots erupt from the earth in late March or April, pale, grey and fleshy. Flowers and foliage appear simultaneously, pale pinkish-white buds thrusting from the centre of rolled leaves. The flowers,

Illustration: *Sanguinaria canadensis* 'Plena'

up to 2in/5cm across, borne on pink-tinged stems, are the purest white, with pointed well separated petals and upright lemon yellow stamens. The leaves – wonderfully ornamental in their own right – are strikingly lobed like those of a miniature fig, glaucous green and deeply veined. In its native habitat bloodroot ranges widely from Florida in the south to Canada in the north and it flourishes in very different soils from the slightly alkaline to the strongly acid. It is a woodland plant and in the garden it must have at the very least part shade. It demands moist, rich soil with plenty of leafmould if possible. Here it will make an excellent companion for other woodland plants – with choice ferns, Solomon's Seal and trilliums. Even more beautiful than the type is a cultivar with fully double flowers, *S. canadensis* 'Plena', which is among the most exquisite of all woodland plants. A rare pink cultivar, *S. canadensis* 'Roseum', has the palest pink single flowers and its foliage is flushed with a dusty mauve. The rhizomes of bloodroot should be planted a good 4in/10cm deep. They are best planted in the autumn which is also the season for dividing over-crowded clumps. They may also be propagated by seed.

Schizostylis

There is just one species of schizostylis, a rhizome in the family Iridaceae.

Schizostylis coccinea
Origin: Southern Africa
Z: 6

❧ The Kaffir Lily, producing its cheerful flowers in late summer or early autumn is one of the most unexpected of bulbous plants. The single flowers are carried at the tips of thin wire-like stems up to 18in/45cm high. The flowers are red, varying in intensity and sometimes with a hint of orange. The petals are veined in a deeper colour and the stamens are unusually long and thin. In the wild it is found in damp places, often on the banks of streams. In the garden it will flower best in rich, moist soil in a sunny position. It is wonderful with grey-leafed plants, such as artemisias which late in the summer start to become blowsy and sprawling making a good background its sprightly colour. It is easy to propagate by dividing the rhizomes in the spring. There is a good white form, *S. coccinea alba*, and many cultivars: *S. coccinea* 'Jennifer' has good pale pink flowers with petals that are wider than the type; *S. coccinea* 'Major' has larger flowers which are rich red.

Scilla

There are about 90 species of scillas, all bulbs, in the family Hyacinthaceae/Liliaceae.

Scilla liliohyacinthus
Origin: France, Spain
Z: 6

❧ The Pyrenean squill combines decorative foliage with flowers of distinctive colour. They appear simultaneously in late April or May – the leaves are broad, strap-like, mid-green with a lustrous surface.

The flowers rise above, held in little umbels, each flower a diminutive pale violet star with deep purple anthers. In the wild it is found in meadows and woods – often as high as 7,000ft/2,000m. In the garden it is very versatile. In would look lovely in a meadow garden or orchard provided the grass has been kept fairly short – the flowering stems rise no more than 4in/10cm. The right sort of place would be where the grass has been cut late in the previous season, for example to display *Cyclamen coum* and *Anemone blanda*. There is an attractive rare, white cultivar, *S. liliohyacinthus* 'Album'.

Scilla messeniaca
Origin: Greece
Z: 8

❧ The Greek squill comes from the Kalamata region, famous for producing the finest olives, and it does indeed look very beautiful growing beneath the silver leaves of olive trees. The flowers in March are borne in little racemes, a beautiful grey-blue, carried on stems that rise to 4in/10cm high. The leaves are quite broad, strap-like, with a gleaming surface. This is a plant for naturalising so that it forms a spreading carpet below other plants. It looks beautiful with the cream-green of the flowers of the Corsican hellebore, *Helleborus argutifolius*. In the wild it likes shady places and is often found growing in pastures. It makes a distinguished underplanting to such spring flowering shrubs as *Corylopsis pauciflora* with whose soft yellow flowers it goes admirably. Some of the smaller, simpler narcissi with creamy yellow flowers also make admirable partners.

Scilla mischtschenkoana
(syn. *S. tubergeniana*)
Origin: Iran, Russia
Z: 6

❧ The first sign of this little bulb is the emerging flower heads – a vigorous froth of blossom – bursting from the soil in February. The flowers are either the palest blue or white, with deep blue veins down the back of each, carried in loose racemes, rising to 3–4in/8–10cm high. They are closely followed by shining, strap-like leaves, to 6in/15cm long. It is best in rich, moist soil, and in order that it should flower as early as possible, plant it in a sunny position. It seeds itself, and clumps may be divided, and it makes an excellent plant for naturalising at the feet of deciduous shrubs such as magnolias which will provide dry summer conditions for its period of dormancy.

Scilla peruviana
Origin: W. Mediterranean
Z: 8

❧ Despite its name this splendid bulb has nothing to do with Peru. It flowers in May or June, producing bold clusters of up to fifty flowers forming a rounded cushion. The buds are a rich, deep purple before they open into violet-blue star-shaped flowers with brilliant

yellow anthers at the centre. The flower heads are
carried on fleshy stems, up to 10in/25cm tall, which rise
above prolific shining leaves. It needs a sunny position
and looks beautiful planted with smaller silver-leafed
shrubs such as santolina (*Santolina chamaecyparissus*).
There are paler coloured forms, including some that are
an almost grey-violet, and a dazzling white cultivar,
S. peruviana 'Alba'.

Scilla siberica
Origin: Armenia, Georgia,
Turkey
Z: 5

❧ This is variable in colour and the best clones have
flowers of a rich vivid blue with a hint of violet. The
leaves are fleshy with a lustrous surface and the flowers,
which open in March, are held at the tips of stems up to
4in/10cm high. The flowers are borne singly, hanging
downwards like slightly crumpled lamp-shades,
marked on the backs of their petals with a dark stripe.
It adds dabs of brilliant colour to the early spring scene,
mingling well with other ornamental planting. In my
garden it grows in a narrow west-facing bed among the

silvery patterned leaves of *Cyclamen hederifolium*. It is at its best with plants of similar small size, such as *Anemone blanda* and *Crocus tommasinianus* with whose grey-violet it looks lovely.

Sisyrinchium

There are about 90 species of sisyrinchium in the family Iridaceae widely distributed in America and Australasia.

Sisyrinchium striatum
Origin: S. America
Z: 8

❧ It is easy to overlook the great merits of this common plant. Its stiff blade-like leaves are evergreen and very ornamental, grey-green in colour and rising to 18in/45cm, providing crisp architectural shape in the blur of a modest border. The flowers in June are an excellent colour, the softest creamy-yellow which harmonises easily with other colours. They are carried in profuse groups on erect stems, each flower like a widely open trumpet, emerging from curiously striped buds. *S. striatum* 'Aunt May' (sometimes wrongly called *S. striatum variegatum*) has especially distinguished leaves striped with swathes of creamy yellow. It is short lived but easily propagated by division in the autumn A sisyrinchium of unknown origins is the cultivar with the very odd name, *Sisyrinchium* 'Quaint and Queer' which has flowers that are cream and ochre, a charming mixture.

Smilacina

There are 25 species of smilacina, all rhizomes, in the family Convallariaceae/Liliaceae, native to Asia and America. They are sometimes called False Solomon's Seal but the species I describe below is entirely distinctive.

Smilacina racemosa
Origin: Central and North America
Z: 4

Among woodland plants this is one of the true aristocrats. Its common name is False Spikenard – a reference to its aromatic qualities which were thought to make it a substitute for the exotic true spikenard, an Indian plant used to make a costly ointment. The leaves are strikingly ornamental, 6in/15cm long, undulating and furrowed, a fresh pale green in colour. Their stems

Illustration:
Smilacina stellata

tend to flop sideways making the foliage resemble a
lively sea of leaves. The flowers which appear at the tips
of the stems in May are airy plumes, creamy white in
colour tinged with green, and giving off a delicious
sweet scent. In warm climates red berries are formed.
This is a superb plant for a shady place, especially
among large shrubs or trees in a woodland garden. It
will spread to form an emphatic clump, rising
36in/90cm high. It needs a cool, shady position in
lime-free soil. It may be propagated by division in the
autumn. It has a much smaller cousin, *S. stellata* (syn.
Maianthemum stellata), which has charm but spreads
like wildfire so should be admitted only to the wildest
corner of the garden.

Sternbergia

There are about seven species of sternbergia in the
family Amaryllidaceae. They are sometimes
referred to as 'autumn daffodil' which is not helpful as,
although they are related, they do not in the slightest
resemble daffodils.

Sternbergia candida
Origin: Turkey
Z: 7

❧ This spring-flowering sternbergia was discovered
only twenty years ago and it was recently in the news
because it has been over collected in the wild. However,
it is now available commercially and well worth
obtaining. The white flowers are carried at the tips of
6in/15cm high flowering stems which rise slightly
higher than the grey-green strap-like foliage which
appears at the same time. The flowers resemble those of

a crocus but in full sun open fully and the petals separate giving the flower the appearance of an irregular star. In the wild it is found in dry, rocky places and on the edge of woodland. In the garden it should have a sunny site and good drainage.

Sternbergia lutea
Origin: Southern Europe
Z: 7

❧ There are very few plants in my garden that give more pleasure. In September or October the flowers erupt from the ground, luminous pale golden yellow, resembling a well-fed crocus, and rising 6in/15cm, looking wonderful among the first autumn leaves. The flowers never open out fully, always remaining slightly cupped even in bright sunshine. When the sun is not shining they are smoothly goblet-shaped. The leaves appear at the same time, lustrous green and strap-like, rising higher than the flowers. The foliage remains throughout the winter, dying in the following spring. It is said to flower best where the bulbs are constricted. Although some authorities say that it needs good drainage my plants flourish in our heavy clay, growing between old paving stones where they seem to relish the moisture. *S. lutea* ssp. *sicula* is very similar but more delicately formed as is *S. colchiciflora* which has more separate and pointed petals.

Tecophilaea

There are two species of *Tecophilaea* in the family Tecophilaeaceae/Liliaceae, both corms. They are native to the high Andes in Chile, found as high as 10,000ft/3,000m.

Tecophilaea cyanocrocus
Origin: Chile
Z: 9

❧ The Chilean crocus, probably extinct in the wild, is creeping back into cultivation through the efforts of conservation botanists. There are plans to reintroduce communities to the wild and it is now available through a few nurseries in Europe and the U.S.A. It is one of the most memorable of all small bulbs. The flowers, which appear in February or March, are of the most intense blue, equalled only by the blue of gentians. The flowers, up to 1 1/2in/3cm long, are loosely trumpet-shaped at first but soon open out fully and a paler throat is revealed, with veins running along the inside of the petals. The leaves are pale green and rise higher than the flowers which are half concealed by the foliage. In its native habitat a carpet of snow protects the Chilean crocus from the harsh winter conditions and it flowers in late autumn. In gardens with a temperate climate the best results will be obtained in a very sunny site in areas of low rainfall where it will flower in late winter or early spring – February to March. It has been successfully grown out of doors in gardens in the south of England in on the east coast of Ireland. It is a plant of such beauty that in less favourable climates it would be worth growing in a cold frame, or Alpine house, for the exhilaration of its dazzling colour. There are two cultivars: *T. cyanocrocus* 'Leichtlinii' with paler blue flowers, not as exciting as the type; and *T. cyanocrocus*. 'Violacea' with deep violet flowers – a good colour but without the piercing intensity of the type.

Tradescantia

There are about 70 species of tradescantia in the family Commelinaceae all native to America. Their name comes from the English royal gardener John Tradescant the Younger who made plant-hunting expeditions to Virginia in the mid 17th century, introducing several North American plants to English gardens.

Tradescantia virginiana
Origin: Eastern U.S.A.
Z: 7

The spider lily is a long-flowering rhizome with striking foliage. The stems bearing leaves and flowers are jointed rather like a reed with leaves sticking out more or less horizontally. These are up to 10in/25cm long, narrow, pointed and with a pleat down the middle. Bunches of flower buds appear cupped between two leaves at the tips of the stems. The flowers which open in May are three-petalled, rounded, and varying in colour – white, blue or purple. In my own garden I have a clone that is white faintly flushed with pale blue. The yellow anthers are suspended above curious hairy sepals as fine as swan's down. It will form a bold upright plant up to 24in/60cm tall with the flowers half-concealed among the leaves. It is best in rich, heavy soil and will flower equally well in sun or part shade. It is easy to propagate by dividing clumps in the autumn. There is a group of cultivars of the hybrid *T. × andersoniana* which include 'J.C. Weguelin' with clear lavender flowers and a good white-flowered one, 'Osprey'. All these are valuable border plants

Tricyrtis

There are about 15 species of tricyrtis, or toad-lilies as they are called, all rhizomatous perennials, in the family Convallariaceae/Liliaceae.

Tricyrtis formosana
Origin: Taiwan
Z: 7

❧ This very decorative perennial is a valuable plant for the late summer border. It flowers in August or September but long before that its distinctive foliage has made its presence felt. The leaves are pointed, rounded, furrowed and their bases are transfixed by the stiff flower stem which rises to a height of 36in/90cm. The flowers are wonderfully exotic. The outer petals are narrow and pointed, white but scattered with spots of deep red. The inner petals have the same colouring but are arranged like a miniature palm-tree or gushing water jet in the centre of the flower which is marked with yellow at its base. The stems and flower-buds are covered with fine hairs. It grows and flowers well in semi-shade and is best in rich, moist soil. I have it mixed, accidentally, with some rather shrill border phlox, pink and carmine, with which it makes a cheerful mixture. It is easy to propagate by dividing the rhizomes in the spring. A separate group, known as Stolonifera Group, has more lax growth, softer foliage and more spots of colour. A cultivar of unknown origin, *T.* 'White Towers' has white flowers and grey-green foliage. *T.* 'Tojen' has solid pink flowers.

Tricyrtis hirta
Origin: Japan
Z: 5

❧ This Japanese toad lily has flowering stems that rise to 36in/90cm with flowers that are similarly elaborate as those of *T. formosana* but they are borne in the leaf axils and the petals are more upright. They are white and have maroon spots. The foliage is striking, boldly heart-shaped and sticking out horizontally from the stem. It is best in dappled-shade in rich, moist soil. There is an admirable white form, *T. hirta alba*, which occasionally has the odd spot of colour. In its native Japan it has been subject to much breeding and there are several cultivars. *T. hirta* 'Miyazaki' has cheerful gold variegated foliage.

Trillium

The wake robins are rhizomatous plants of which there are about 30 species in the family Trilliaceae/Liliaceae. They are native to North America and Asia. They derive their scientific name from the three-part division of foliage and flowers which they all have. Many gardeners have had difficulty in getting these lovely plants established. The best advice is to buy them from a specialist nursery run by people who understand their needs; never touch those miserable dried-out rhizomes, from dubious sources, sometimes seen in garden centres. They may be propagated by division in the autumn, adding enriched soil. For more intrepid gardeners, they may also be propagated by seed, but it is unlikely that plants will flower in less than four or five years. Most prefer acid soil but a few demand alkaline.

Trillium chloropetalum
Origin: W. U.S.A.
Z: 6

🐚 Some trilliums give off a pungent smell – one of their common names is stinking Benjamin – but this one has the most delicious, and unexpected, scent of roses. The flowers, which appear in April, vary in colour from deep red to white. The most beautiful of all is a lovely pale rosy purple. The leaves, up to 6in/15cm across, are particularly decorative, with pale veins and scatterings of dark marbling. They are rather upright and slightly cupped, forming a graceful frame for the exquisite flowers. A site that is at least semi-shaded is needed, with moist, rich soil that is neutral or alkaline. It is beautiful underplanted with smaller bulbous plants that also have decorative foliage such as erythroniums and *Cyclamen hederifolium*.

Trillium cuneatum
Origin: S.E. U.S.A.
Z: 6

The flowers of this is among the largest and stateliest of the trilliums with the fleshy stems rising as tall as 24in/60cm. The leaves are in proportion, with each of the three parts 4in/10cm long, making a bold shape, deeply veined with dark mottled marbling. The wedge-shaped flowers in April are a marvellous deep purple-black with an intricate pattern of almost black veins. This is one of the grandest of woodland plants and it is well worth lavishing on it the care which it demands. It needs humus-rich soil that never dries out but nor should it ever be water-logged. In the wild it is found in shady places in alkaline or neutral soil. A deep mulch of the best compost you can lay your hands on will help it to thrive. In the garden find a position that will provide shade when the trilliums are in leaf. A good place is underneath substantial spring-flowering deciduous shrubs such as corylopsis, hydrangeas, magnolias and viburnums.

Trillium erectum
Origin: E. North America
Z: 4

The flowers of this trillium, which open in April, are among the most beautiful of the genus. They vary in colour but the very best are blood red etched with veins in an even deeper colour. The petals are rounded and pointed and their tips curve back sharply and the stamens are pale yellow. The foliage is rounded, a fresh mid green with pale veins, with a lustrous surface. It rises to a height of about 18in/45cm and has an air of the greatest distinction. *T. erectum albiflorum* has white flowers flushed with green and *T. erectum luteum* has a yellowish leaf stalk and rich red flower.

Trillium grandiflorum
Origin: E. North America
Z: 5

This forms a burgeoning mound of foliage with profusely borne flowers. The leaves are especially attractive, deeply veined, twisting and creating a lively background to the flowers. These, appearing in April or May, are of a dazzling white, strikingly furrowed, set off by cheerful lemon-yellow stamens. It will form a shapely clump up to 18in/45cm high and must have a position that is at least partly shaded. It makes a wonderful underplanting to flowering shrubs; I have seen it beautifully used spreading underneath a

Illustration opposite:
Trillium cuneatum

Illustration:
Trillium grandiflorum

Magnolia stellata, producing its flowers as the last of
the magnolia fade. The flowers are variable: there is an
exceptionally beautiful double-flowered form,
T. grandiflorum flore-pleno; and a rarely seen pink
cultivar, *T. grandiflorum* 'Roseum', which is richly
coloured with striking deeper-coloured veins. In its
native habitat *T. grandiflorum* is found in limestone and
is thus one of the few trilliums that will flourish in very
alkaline soil.

Trillium ludovicianum
Origin: S.E. U.S.A.
Z: 6

❧ This is a rarity – but it is well worth seeking out.
The leaves are particularly beautiful, up to 6in/15cm
long, oval, with an undulating margin. They are
especially handsomely marked with dark green
marbling and a network of paler veins. The leaves are
held well up on stems up to 15in/35cm tall. The flowers
are a lovely glowing, rich red with green sepals striped
with red – they have a vague whiff of dirty socks. It
flowers in April and makes one of the most ornamental
of all its tribe. The oval fruit are a striking pale purple

colour. In the wild it grows in rich, moist soil in forests or shady places by the banks of rivers. If you can find a similar position in your garden there are few plants more worthwhile to grow.

Trillium ovatum
Origin: W. North America
Z: 5

❧ This beautiful trillium has especially elegant flowers well carried above spreading foliage. They appear in April or May, with petals separate, white, with undulating margins and a flush of rosy pink. As the flowers age the pink begins to suffuse the whole flower, with deeper coloured veins becoming more visible. They are held on 4in/10cm red-brown fleshy stems above the foliage which is low lying, spreading across the surface of the ground. In the wild this is a plant of coniferous forest and a shady position will suit it best in the garden. In appropriate conditions it makes admirable floriferous ground cover, the foliage remaining attractive long after the flowers have gone.

Trillium pusillum
Origin: E. U.S.A.
Arkansas, Missouri, Texas
Z: 6

❧ This little trillium is quite unlike any other species. It stands very upright with flowers and sepals at the tip of fleshy stems which are up to 12in/30cm high. The base of the stems is a dark purple, becoming green farther up. The flowers in April are white, or the palest pink, with prominent pale lemon yellow anthers. In the wild it is found on dry wooded slopes and in low woodlands of the coastal plains. Plants from the western states are slightly larger than those from the east which are sometimes seen listed as *T. pusillum* var. *virginicum*. I have seen it grown very well on scree in a rock garden. It would be a lovely ornament of a shady, woodland area where it should be planted in a bold clump – the flowers, which are rather small in relation to the height of the plant, look best in a group.

Trillium rivale
Origin: W. U.S.A.
Z: 4

❧ This is one of the smaller trilliums, with flowering stems no more than 4in/10cm long. The flowers are variable in colour from white to pale pink – the most desirable are handsomely freckled within with purple spots. Like all trilliums the flowers have the three-part division of petals but here they are so neatly overlapped as to form a cupped circle. The leaves, on the other hand, are widely separated, rounded and pointed, with the flowers held well above. Despite its exquisite delicacy *T. rivale* is found in harsh conditions in its native habit – in mountainous regions as high as 4,000ft/1,200m and in coniferous woodland. In the garden it will do best in part-shade in rich soil. It grows particularly well in the cooler gardens of Scotland. It is one of those plants whose greatest virtue is its own distinctive beauty rather than in its ability to mix with others. It is an admirable rock-garden plant and I have also seen it looking very beautiful spreading out at the foot of a strawberry tree, *Arbutus unedo*.

Trillium sessile
Origin: N.E. United States
Z: 4

❧ Sessile means stalk-less which in this case refers to the flower which sits neatly with its base hard against the foliage underneath – like something delicious sitting on a plate. The flowers appearing in April are a dazzling apparition – a rich deep maroon with a glistening surface and framed in green-purple outer petals. They are shown off to marvellous advantage by the leaves which are up to 4in/10cm across, pale green but richly mottled with darker green markings, creating a sumptuous effect. The whole plant stands no more than 12in/30cm high. In the wild it is found in alkaline soil and like other trilliums needs moist humus-rich soil in the shade. It is wonderful with Lenten hellebores (*Helleborus orientalis*) whose flowers will be fading just as the trilliums come into full beauty. The cultivar *T. sessile* 'Rubrum' has resplendent flowers of a more crimson colour.

Triteleia

There are about 15 species of triteleia, all corms, in the family Alliaceae/Liliaceae. The genus has been a botanist's battlefield with species transferred from one genus to another. Some species of *Triteleia* are now *Ipheion* or *Dichelostemma*.

Illustration: *Triteleia* 'Koningin Fabiola'

Triteleia laxa
Origin: California, Oregon
Z: 7

❧ Previously known as *Brodiaea laxa*, this summer-flowering plant is of the kind that illuminates odd corners of the garden, adding just those decorative details that give character. It flowers in June or July, with umbels of upward-pointing little trumpets of violet-blue or white. Each flower is carried on a long stalk and the whole umbel is held on a wiry stem about 12in/30cm high. It takes up practically no ground space and the flowers rise above lower plantings and dance in the breeze. It thrives in quite poor soil and needs a sunny position. In these conditions it will seed itself happily (but not *too* happily). It may also be propagated by dividing clumps of corms in early spring. Corms should be planted 4in/10cm deep. It is an excellent front-of-the-border plant which may also be planted in places too small to allow other plants. An admirable cultivar, *T. laxa* 'Koningin Fabiola' (or 'Queen Fabiola'), has rich coloured purple-blue flowers borne in great profusion.

Tropaeolum

There are about 80 species of tropaeolum in the family Tropaeolaceae, all native to South America. Among them is the common annual nasturtium, *T. majus.*

Tropaeolum speciosum
Origin: Chile
Z: 7

❧ This enchanting plant is well-known to be difficult to establish and, once established, to wander in unpredictable places. It seems to prefer cool, damp places and in Britain is always seen at its best in the north of England and in Scotland. It is a rhizomatous climbing plant which scrambles through other plants casting a veil of dazzling scarlet flowers in June or July wherever it goes – rising to at least 10ft/3m. The flowers are like diminutive nasturtiums, trumpet-shaped with a sharp spur behind. They have yellow veins at the base and yellow stamens, and are carried on plum-coloured stems. The flowers are followed by rich blue berries. The foliage is also decorative, with glaucous lobed leaves. It is most commonly seen on yew hedges where the dark green makes a superb background. Although most frequently seen in gardens of acid soil it will grow perfectly well, with plenty of humus, in calcareous soil. It seems to establish itself best in a shady, rather dry place such as at the base of a yew hedge. It has a natural tendency to establish itself on the cooler side of its host plant. It may be propagated by dividing rhizomes in the spring.

Tropaeolum tuberosum
Origin: Bolivia, Peru
Z: 8

This tuberous climbing nasturtium has a splendid combination of orange-yellow flowers and glaucous grey leaves. The flowers are similar to those of *T. speciosum* but neater. They are warm orange on the outside and yellow-orange within, opening in late summer and continuing well into the autumn. The attractive lobed leaves appear well before the flowers. It must have a sunny position and is in any case not a plant for cold gardens. It will flower best scrambling through other plants on a south-facing wall where it will rise to at least 10ft/3m. It should have rich, moist soil. It is a marvellous climber to provide flowering ornament in a season when most clematis and roses have ceased to flower. It looks beautiful among the glistening seed-heads of *Clematis orientalis*.

Tulbaghia

Named after an 18th-century Governor of the Cape, Ryk Tulbagh, these attractive bulbs and rhizomes are found only in South Africa where they are known as wild garlic. There are about 25 species, in the family Alliaceae/Liliaceae. Most of the species need a frost-free climate but some, from high mountain sites, may be hardy in temperate gardens in Zone 8. Failing that, they make marvellous plants for pots and troughs, with the added bonus that some species are deliciously scented.

Tulbaghia violacea
Origin: South Africa
Z: 8

This rhizome produces slender glaucous grass-like stems crowned with dazzling umbels of flowers. The flowers in July or August are very elegant – little elongated trumpets, a warm lilac-violet, opening out abruptly, with deeper stripes down the middle of the petals. Each umbel carries up to fifteen flowers which

are sweetly scented. The flowering stems, 24in/60cm high, rise above narrow glaucous leaves – which smell strongly of onion when bruised. This is a plant to be admired for its exquisite detail – form, scent and colour – rather than for its structural presence in a busy border. It must have very sharp drainage and the sunniest position you can find. It is marvellous by itself, in an appropriate little bed or in a pot or trough, or with a carefully chosen partner. I have seen it looking magnificent with the vermilion-flowered *Zauschneria californica* which flowers at the same time. *T. violacea* 'Silver Lace' is a handsome cultivar with variegated leaves, which are grey with a fine edging of silver on each side. It is a most elegant plant, the silver setting off the violet to especially good effect.

Tulipa

The name tulip comes from the Turkish for a turban, *tulbend*, which the flower somewhat resembles. There are about 100 species, in the family Liliaceae/Liliaceae, from the Mediterranean region and Central Asia. Among the first garden plants to be given cultivar names, they have excited the interest of gardeners at least since the 16th century and in the Low Countries in the early 17th century they became the subject of frenzied investment speculation. The market

Illustration opposite:
Tulipa 'Purissima'

Illustration:
Tulipa 'Abu Hassan'

crashed but tulips have remained a Dutch speciality and essential garden plants.

These are the most precious spring-flowering bulbs, with a wide range of colours and shapes. Their flowering period runs through three months, from April to June when the beautiful *T. sprengeri* ends the season with a splendid trumpet blast of brilliant colour. In the garden they have many uses – in the border or meadow garden, in the rockery, alpine trough or other containers. Many make easy association plants and the colours available are so diverse that very specific effects are possible. The more exotic kinds, those with elaborate petals richly splashed or striped with contrasting colours, demand a simple setting.

The vast majority of tulips seen in public places and in gardens are cultivars, so remote from their wild origins that nothing is known of the species from which they derive. I describe below in some detail some of the species many of which – apart from the beauty of their flowers – have the great advantage that they will naturalise in conditions that suit them; almost all modern cultivars are sterile. The cultivars will usually not flower well from year to year unless they are lifted after flowering, stored in a dry place and replanted in the following autumn, even then they will require a further year to produce full-sized flowers.

Illustration:
Tulipa 'Candela'

Those left to struggle, particularly in heavy soil, may rot, are prey to slugs, and the few survivals often produce irritatingly sickly flowers. Many gardeners give up the struggle and regard them as annuals. Others claim that, with good drainage and plenty of lime, they will flourish for years. In my own heavy, wet soil I have never achieved this except in a large old copper. Here, with excellent drainage, a group of the yellow lily-flowered 'Candela' has formed a successful colony, flowering regularly for ten years.

Bulbs should be planted between 6in/15cm and 8in/20cm deep, the smaller bulbs (i.e. species) more shallowly than the larger ones. When planting them avoid at all cost any hint of regimentation unless you are planning a severely municipal effect. It will help to achieve naturalistic drifts if you arrange the bulbs on the ground before planting. Late autumn or early winter is the recommended time of planting but some gardeners have reported successes with tulips planted as late as February. If you are planning to encourage a permanent colony, leaves should be left after flowering as they are the channel through which the new bulb receives nourishment. The dying leaves are ugly but may be concealed by the emerging new foliage of neighbouring herbaceous plants.

Tulips have been divided by the Dutch Koninklijke

Illustration: *Tulipa* 'White Triumphator'

Algemeene Vereening voor Bloembollenculture into four groups – Early Flowering, Mid-Season, Late Flowering and Species and their Hybrids. These broad divisions have been broken down into fourteen sections according to the general shape or character of the flowers. The group Species and their Hybrids includes tulips that flower early, mid and late. Those derived from *T. kaufmanniana*, with their characteristically purple-mottled leaves, such as 'Glück', with yellow and scarlet striped flowers, are among the earliest to flower. Hybrids and cultivars of *T. fosteriana* give one of the best yellow single tulips, 'Candela', which flowers in early April; 'Purissima', an excellent white double of the same origin, flowers in early May. The third group of species, derived from *T. greigii*, all flower in the mid season. They have in common purple-marked leaves and rather short, stubby flowers. Most have orange-red flowers and some are striped with yellow. 'Red Riding Hood' is an attractive scarlet one with goblet shaped flowers. The

Illustration:
Tulipa 'Apricot Parrot'

late flowering Lily-Flowered Group, which flowers at the beginning of May, provides some of the most beautiful cultivars. They have in common long, elegantly-shaped flowers with pointed petals. 'China Pink' is a good warm pink; 'White Triumphator' is one of the best of all the single whites, eventually opening its petals into widely-spreading wings; 'West Point' is a fine clear yellow with strikingly pointed petals which reflex backwards. The Viridiflora Group, as the name implies, have flowers flushed with green: 'Spring Green' flowering in early May has pale yellow flowers suffused with lime-green making it a particularly good ingredient of a white, yellow and green arrangement. 'Mount Tacoma', flowering at the same time, is a fine double-flowered white. The Parrot Tulips, all late-flowering, evoke the most lavishly exotic blooms of 17th-century tulipomania. Some have flower-heads so large and heavy as to cause them to flop over. Many are irresistibly over the top – such as 'Apricot Parrot' with pleated and frilled petals suffused with apricot, pink and cream like some stupendous sundae. 'Black Parrot', on the other hand, is an exceptional Satanic purple of the deepest colouring, wonderful with pale grey foliage – I have seen it lookinmg superb among the silver foliage of cardoons, *Cynara cardunculus.*

Tulipa clusiana var. chrysantha
Origin: Garden
Z: 5

Tulipa clusiana is named after the great botanist Carolus Clusius who, in the second half of the 16th century, was one of the first to study bulbs systematically. The flowers of the variety *T. clusiana* var. *chrysantha* open in April and are a rich golden yellow (rather than the white of *T. clusiana*) and marked on the back of the petals with red smudges. It rises to about 10in/25cm tall, and the newly opened flower has upright heads with crisply pointed petals but as it ages the flower heads flop and the petals twist creating a splendidly languid effect. It is best in sun in sharply drained soil where many gardeners have found it will establish itself well.

Tulipa kaufmanniana
Origin: Central Asia
Z: 5

This March-flowering tulip is a marvellous spring plant. The flowers are creamy yellow with a rich golden centre and in full sunshine they open very widely, with the petals quite separate. The backs of the petals are marked with red and the foliage is especially attractive with broad, glaucous green, undulating leaves. As many as five flowers are carried on each stem which rises to a height of 8in/20cm. In the wild it is found in dry, stony places, quite high up. In the garden it should have a sunny, well-drained site where, in its summer dormancy, it can dry out completely. The front of a south-facing border, covered later in the season by the foliage of other plants, is a good place.

Tulipa linifolia
Origin: Central Asia
Z: 5

❧ This little tulip, rising no more than 6in/15cm high, has an exceptionally distinguished character. The leaves are narrow, folded down the centre, a lustrous green edge with fine red margins. The flowers start to open when they are still shrouded by the foliage, showing a dazzling scarlet. When they open fully in May the pointed petals spread sideways giving a more dishevelled appearance and revealing black splotches at the base of the petals. In the wild it is found high up in the mountains in dry, stony areas. In the garden it makes an excellent front-of-the-border ornament in a sunny place with excellent drainage. Here it may well settle down and form a self-perpetuating colony. The colour associates especially well with silver-leafed shrubs of Mediterranean character such as lavender, santolina or small-leafed sage.

Tulipa marjolettii
Origin: S. Europe
Z: 6

❧ This is a valuable little tulip which will settle down and multiply with ease. It produces its flowers in early May, a warm creamy yellow with variable red edgings to some of the petals. As the flowers age they take on the colouring of a ripe yellow peach. The flower remains shapely, never spreading its petals fully open. It will grow 9in/23cm high and makes a good companion for other low-growing plants that perform in the same season such as the smaller bearded irises (especially pale blue ones), forget-me-nots and the chalky-blue *Veronica gentianoides*. I have seen it looking marvellous growing through the finely cut foliage of *Dicentra formosa* 'Stuart Boothman' whose pale salmon coloured flowers make a pretty accompaniment. Although some authorities say that it needs a sunny position and sharp drainage, I grow it successfully in half-shade in heavy soil.

Tulipa orphanidea
Origin: Balkan Peninsula
Z: 5

❧ The colour of this tulip is as close as nature gets to producing an orange flower. The flowers, which appear in late April or May are at first rounded and pointed but open out into a cupped shape, resembling a miniature water-lily. The colour is variable from red-brown to a marvellous rusty-red but always with a soft stripe of yellow on the inside of the petals and a

Illustration opposite:
Tulipa saxatilis

yellow flush to the outside. The centre of the flower is black with deep purple anthers. This is one of the prettiest of all the wild tulips, with its flowers held high on thin stems 6in/10cm long. The leaves are a pale, glaucous grey. In the wild it is found in damp meadows and rocky places in the mountains. In the garden it should have a sunny position in humus-rich soil.
T. whittallii is either a synonym or a slightly shorter version of exactly the same thing.

Tulipa praestans
Origin: Central Asia
Z: 5

❧ In my garden this is the first tulip to flower, opening in late March or April, and providing an exhilarating jolt of red when everything else in the garden seems green, yellow or blue. The single flowers are held on stems 7in/18cm tall, opening to show a splendid rich scarlet, with decorative glaucous grey foliage below. A slightly larger cultivar, *T. praestans* 'Van Tubergen's Variety', has a hint of orange in the scarlet. It should have a well-drained position in the sun and it looks especially beautiful against the silver-grey foliage of such small shrubs as santolina. The foliage is a decorative glaucous grey.

Tulipa saxatilis
Origin: Crete, Turkey
Z: 6

❧ The flowers of *T. saxatilis* open in April, pale lilac pink with a striking yellow smudge at the base of each petal – as though dipped in gold-dust. The petals are pointed and the flower stems are 8in/20cm long. It is one of the most striking and elegant of the species

tulips. *T. bakeri* is similar but smaller, only 6in/15cm high, and with a deeper lilac-purple colour of flower which somewhat resembles a tall crocus. Both these demand a warm, sunny position and excellent drainage.

Tulipa sprengeri
Origin: Turkey
Z: 5

❧ Flowering well into June *Tulipa sprengeri* gives the tulip season a triumphant send off. It is among the most decorative of all, a dazzling blood-red flower carried on a stem up to 12in/30cm high. The petals are long and pointed with a hint of pale yellow on the outside and brilliant yellow anthers within. The foliage is a fresh green with a lustrous texture. This is one of the tulips which gardeners find most easy to naturalise. It will seed itself with abandon – indeed some lucky gardeners have complained of having too much of it. It is said to do well in sun or shade, in peat or dry soil. I have seen it in a sunny courtyard having sown itself liberally along the cracks between paving stones. It looks wonderful in a sunny border with small shrubs like cistus, lavender and thyme. I have seen it brilliantly planted with the silver-pink cistus 'Peggy Sammons' among whose lower branches it threaded its way.

Tulipa sylvestris
Origin: European
Mediterranean
Z: 5

ᨠ This European wild tulip is of slightly mysterious origin. It is now fairly wildly naturalised in many lowland areas. It is a marvellous garden plant for it has much of the brilliance of the cultivars with all the charm and grace of the species. It flowers in April, the flower buds swaying on tall, thin stems up to 12in/30cm high, marked with a slight bronze tinge. The flowers when fully open are a sprightly yellow, sweetly scented and the petals are rounded and pointed – some of them curling backwards gracefully. It is a good tulip for naturalising, in sun or semi-shade. Plant it under spring-flowering deciduous shrubs and trees such as *Viburnum carlesii* or *Amelanchier canadensis*.

T. sylvestris ssp. *australis* is almost identical but on a much more delicate scale, growing no more than 9in/23cm tall and with narrower flowers whose petals are smudged with green on their backs. It has very slender stems which allow the flowers to sway elegantly in the slightest breeze.

Tulipa tarda
Origin: Central Asia
Z: 5

❧ Despite its name this is one of the earlier flowering tulips. The flowers open in April, white with a lemon centre. As many as eight flowers are produced on each bulb and a good clump gives a wonderful impression of floriferous abundance with flowers packed together among the distinguished glaucous green foliage. The buds are very elegant before opening, long and pointed with a smudge of green down the back of each petal. The flowering stems are no more than 6in/15cm long. This is a good tulip for naturalising in a sunny, rather dry place. I grew it successfully on a south-facing slope, where in a warm spring it would flower as early as March. Here it intermingled with *Crocus tommasinianus* and stars of Bethlehem (*Ornithogalum umbellatum*) making a lovely spring mixture.

Uvularia

Uvularia grandiflora
Origin: S.E. U.S.A.
Z: 4

There are about five species of uvularia, all rhizomes, in the family Convallariaceae/Liliaceae.

❧ Any gardener who can provide the right conditions for this lovely plant should do so. Its stems thrust through the earth in the early spring looking very much like those of its close relation, Solomon's Seal. The leaves are pale green and lightly furrowed. The flowers which open in March or April are a beautiful

crisp lemon yellow, hanging downwards, up to 2in/5cm long, and half-concealed among the foliage. The petals twist slightly and their bases are striped with green. A colony of *Uvularia grandiflora* makes a dazzling sight, with the stems rising as high as 30in/75cm and the mass of twisting leaves creating a lively pattern. In the wild it grows in light acid soil but it will grow in neutral soil. It is at its best in shade or part-shade and makes a wonderful underplanting for larger shrubs in the naturalistic setting of a woodland garden. It is also an admirable companion for other herbaceous plants, such as ferns, hellebores and pulmonarias which need the same conditions. It may be propagated by dividing the rhizomes in autumn.

Veratrum

Veratrum album
Origin: Europe, N. Africa, Siberia
Z: 5

Illustration opposite:
Veratrum album

The name comes from the Latin for 'truly black' – a reference to the plants' dark rhizomes. There are about 25 species, in the family Melanthaceae/Liliaceae, all native to areas with temperate climates.

❧ The most dazzling quality of the false helleborine is its resplendent foliage which unfurls from the ground in April, curved and intricately pleated like rare and wonderful fabric. These are up to 12in/30cm long, gracefully rounded and coming to an unexpected point. The flowers merge in June, tall racemes of green white flowers, forming a stately spire of green and cream up to 24in/60cm high which would be more impressive if the leaves were not so striking. These form a beautiful background for other herbaceous plantings in the spring – tulips and primulas are good companions. It should be given a sunny site in rich moisture-retentive soil. Later in the summer the leaves lose their freshness and become rather tatty. If possible try and plant it so that other plants – perhaps geraniums or the larger campanulas – will grow up to conceal this defect. It is best propagated by dividing the rhizomes in the autumn; seeds germinate easily but it takes four or five years to produce flowering plants.

Zantedeschia

Zantedeschia aethiopica
Origin: South Africa
Z: 8

There are five species of arum lily in the family Araceae. They are all rhizomes, native to southern Africa.

❧ This is one of the less tender arum lilies which makes a striking ornamental plant. The foliage is magnificent, large loosely arrow-shaped leaves of a dark green colour, with a glossy surface and undulating margins. The flowers, with white spathes shaped like irregular trumpets, open in June from curious twisting lime-green buds. It will grow to about 4ft/1.2m high. In growth it needs much water and is at its best in a shady position in very rich soil. In less favoured climates it makes a superlative pot plant but it will need very rich, moisture-retentive compost and watering at

least daily in warm weather. It may be propagated by removing suckers in spring. *Z. aethiopica* 'Crowborough' is almost identical but will flourish in much drier conditions. *Z. aethiopica* 'Green Goddess' has striking mysteriously green spathes and is hardier than the type.

Zephyranthes

Zephyranthes candida
Origin: South America
Z: 8

There are about 70 species of zephyranthes in the family Amaryllidaceae/Liliaceae.

❧ Flowering towards the end of August, usually when the weather becomes cooler, this very attractive bulb is a welcome surprise. The flowers are white, star shaped with upright pale yellow anthers. The petals have pale grey stripes down their length and their tips are occasionally splashed with pink – which may also be visible on their underside. They are held at the tips of stiff stems, rosy pink where the flower starts. The leaves are very thin, grass like, rising to 12in/30cm, taller than the flowers. In the wild it is found in marshland and in the garden it is said to do best in rich, moist soil. I have seen it flourishing in a rather dry place at the front of a border – at all events, it needs sun.

Bulbs for Different Sites

Bulbs for Shade
Many species of bulbous plants have woodland or shady places as their natural habitat. In the garden they are especially valuable, ornamenting places which may otherwise be difficult to plant.

Allium triquetrum
A. ursinum
Anemone blanda
A. nemorosa
Arum italicum ssp *italicum*
  'Marmoratum'
Cardiocrinum giganteum
Convallaria majalis
Corydalis flexuosa
Cyclamen pupurascens
Disporum flavens
Erythronium species
Fritillaria pallidiflora
Galanthus species and cultivars
Hyacinthoides non-scripta
Iris douglasiana and cultivars
Leucojum vernum

Lilium martagon
L. monadelphum
Nomocharis pardanthina
  punctulata
Polygonatum × *hybridum*
Ranunculus ficaria
Sanguinaria canadensis
Smilacina racemosa
Trillium species
Uvularia grandiflora

Bulbs for Different Sites

Bulbs for Positions in Full Sun

Many bulbs demand a sunny, protected position. In some cases they will do well in quite poor, thin soil but others need both sunshine and a rich, moist soil.

Albuca nelsonii
Alstroemeria haemantha
  A. psittacina
× *Amarcrinum memoria-corsii*
Amaryllis bella-donna
Asphodeline lutea
Asphodelus aestivus
Cosmos atrosanguineus
Crinum bulbispermum
  C. × powellii
Crocus gargaricus
Dahlia species and cultivars
Dichelostemma congestum
  D. ida-maia
Dierama dracomontanum
  D. pendulum
  D. pulcherrimum
Eremurus robustus
Fritillaria assyriaca
  F. michailovskyi
Galtonia species
Geranium tuberosum
Gladiolus callianthus
  G. papilio
  G. 'The Bride'
Iris missouriensis
  I. orientalis
  I. unguicularis
Ixiolirion tataricum
Kniphofia species and cultivars
Libertia formosa

Lilium candidum
  L. longiflorum
  L. speciosum
Moraea huttonii
Nerine bowdenii
Ornithogalum arabicum
Paradisea lusitanica
Rhodohypoxis baurii
Romulea nivalis
Schizostylis coccinea
Tulbaghia violacea
Zephyranthes candida

Bulbs for damp sites

Although many bulbs need rich moisture-retentive soil some are at their best by the banks of streams or pools with the water lapping at their stems

Canna species and cultivars
Dactylorhiza elata
  D. praetermissa
Epipactis palustris
Iris ensata
  I. laevigata

I. orientalis
I. pseudacorus
I. sanguinea
I. sibirica
Zantedeschia aethiopica

Bulbs for Meadows and Orchards

Many bulbs are at their most decorative in naturalistic settings. In meadows or orchards with grass, the important thing is to leave plants until they have set seeds or the foliage has withered before cutting the grass. This may be too late for many people's taste – but the effect is marvellous.

Anemone blanda
Camassia quamash
Cyclamen coum
Fritillaria meleagris
  F. pyrenaica

Hyacinthoides non-scripta
Iris latifolia
Narcissus species and cultivars
Ornithogalum pyrenaicum
Scilla liliohyacinthus

Bulbs for Pots and Containers

Bulbs are in many ways the perfect pot plants. They are easy to move when dormant and, for the trickier kinds, the pot makes it easy to provide exactly the right position and soil.

Albuca nelsonii
× *Amarcrinum memoria-corsii*
Amaryllis bella-donna
Cosmos atrosanguineus
Crinum × *powellii*
Eucomis species
Fritillaria persica
Galtonia candicans

G. regalis
Gladiolus callianthus
  G. papilio
  G. 'The Bride'
Iris species
Lilium species and cultivars
Narcissus species and cultivars
Tulipa species and cultivars

Bulbs with Specific Qualities

Bulbs of Architectural Character

These are bulbs which by virtue of bold shapely foliage or spectacular flowers will make a structural contribution to the garden.

Albuca nelsonii
Allium aflatunense
  A. christophii
  A. nigrum
  A. rosenbachianum
  A. schubertii
× *Amarcrinum memoria-corsii*
Amaryllis bella-donna
Anthericum liliago

Asphodeline lutea
Asphodelus aestivus
  A. albus
Camassia leichtlinii
Canna species and cultivars
Cardiocrinum giganteum
Crinum × *powellii*
Crocosmia species and cultivars
Dactylorhiza elata

245

Plants of Architectural Character (continued)

Dierama pulcherrimum
Dracunculus vulgaris
Eremurus robustus
Eucomis species
Fritillaria imperialis
  F. persica
Galtonia candicans
  G. regalis
Gladiolus communis ssp.
  byzantinus
Hedychium coronarium
Iris magnifica
  I. orientalis
  I. pseudacorus
  I. sanguinea
  I. sibirica
Kniphofia caulescens
  K. uvularia 'Nobilis'
Lilium candidum
  L. longiflorum
  L. martagon
  L. monadelphum
  L. pardalinum
Moraea huttonii
Nectaroscordum siculum

Paradisea lusitanica
Polygonatum × hybridum
Sisyrinchium striatum
Veratrum album

Bulbs with Specific Qualities

Bulbs for Scent

Some bulbs have among the most delicious scent of all plants. Several of those listed here are also suitable for cultivation in pots or containers, making them especially good for terraces or other sitting places were the scent will be particularly appreciated.

Albuca nelsonii
× *Amarcrinum memoria-corsii*
Amaryllis bella-donna
Cardiocrinum giganteum
Convallaria majalis
Cosmos atrosanguineus
Crinum bulbispermum
  C. × *powelli*
Crocus tommasinianus
Cyclamen repandum
Fritillaria michailovskyi
Gladiolus callianthus
Hedychium coronarium
Hemerocallis citrina
  H. lilioasphodelus

Hermodactylus tuberosus
Iris orientalis
  I. unguicularis
Lilium auratum
  L. candidum
  L. longiflorum
  L. regale
  L. speciosum
Muscari macrocarpum
Narcissus jonquilla
  N. papyraceus
  N. poeticus
  N. tazetta
Smilacina racemosa
Tulbaghia violacea

Bulbs with Decorative Foliage

Several bulbs have ornamental foliage, continuing to be ornamental long after flowers have faded. In some cases the foliage becomes more attractive after flowering; in other cases, such as the beautiful *Arum italicum* ssp. *italicum* 'Marmoratum', the foliage is the most beautiful feature.

Allium karataviense
Arum italicum ssp. *italicum*
  'Marmoratum'
Canna species and cultivars
Convallaria majalis
Corydalis flexuosa
  C. lutea
  C. solida
Crinum species
Crocosmia species and cultivars
Cyclamen hederifolium
  C. purpurascens
  C. repandum
Dahlia species and cultivars

Dracunculus vulgaris
Eranthis hyemalis
Erythronium species
Iris pseudacorus
Polygonatum × *hybridum*
Ranunculus ficaria
  'Brazen Hussy'
Sanguinaria canadensis
Smilacina racemosa
Trillium species
Tropaeolum species
Uvularia grandiflora
Veratrum album
Zantedeschia aethiopica

Hardiness Zones

Temperature Ranges		
F	Zone	C
below −50	1	below −45
−50 to −40	2	−45 to −40
−40 to −30	3	−40 to −34
−30 to −20	4	−34 to −29
−20 to −10	5	−29 to −23
−10 to 0	6	−23 to −17
0 to 10	7	−17 to −12
10 to 20	8	−12 to −7
20 to 30	9	−7 to −1
30 to 40	10	−1 to 5

Hardiness zones are based on the average annual minimum temperature in different areas, graded from Zone 1, the coldest, to Zone 10, the warmest; thus, if a plant has the rating Zone 7 it will not dependably survive in a zone of a lower number. But the data are only broadly relevant and are more valid for continental climates than for maritime ones. In Britain and many parts of Europe, for example, local microclimate rather than the hardiness zone band is more likely to determine a plant's hardiness. It should also be said that a plant's chances of survival may be influenced by other things than temperature; drainage, rain, amount of sunshine and protection from winds may make a fundamental difference.

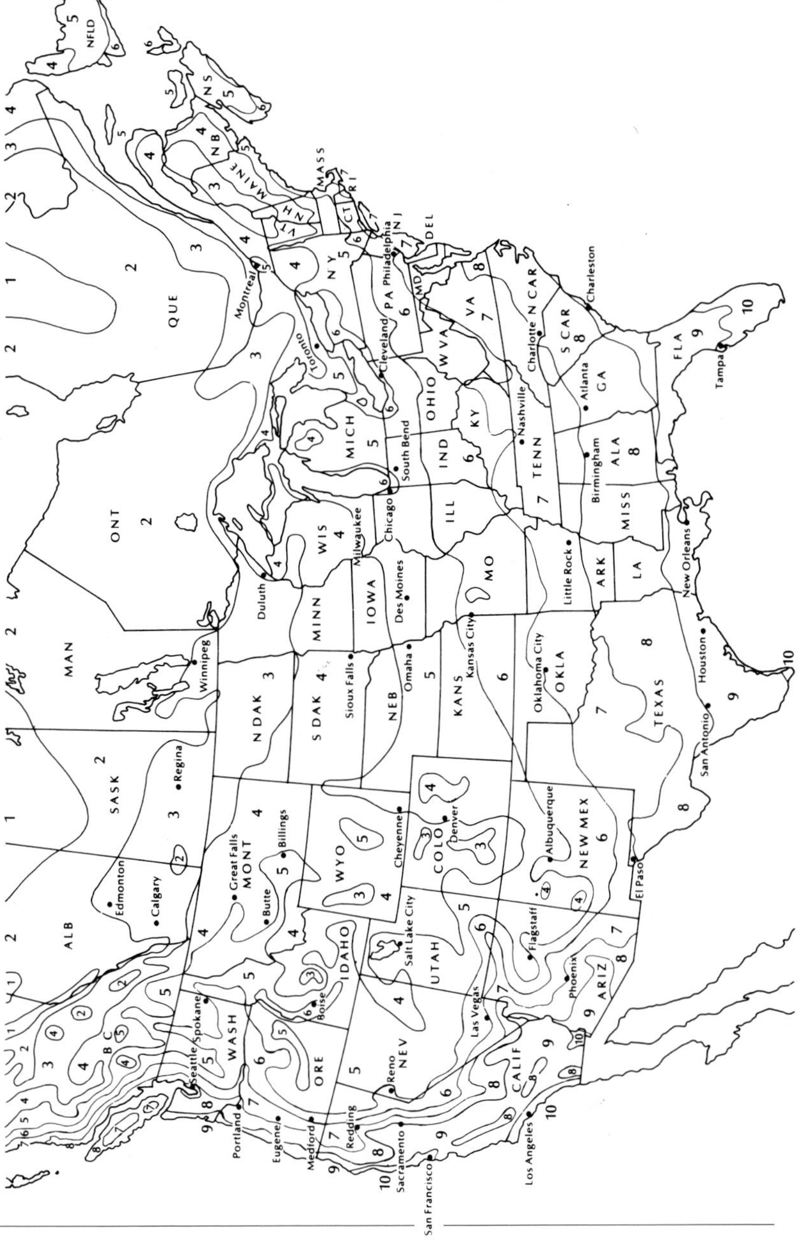

NFLD
N S
N B
QUE
Montreal
MAINE
N H
V T
MASS
R I
CT
N Y
N J
DEL
MD
Philadelphia
PA
Cleveland
Toronto
ONT
MAN
SASK
ALB
B C
Winnipeg
Regina
Edmonton
Calgary
VA
W VA
N CAR
S CAR
Charleston
Charlotte
GA
Atlanta
FLA
Tampa
OHIO
KY
Nashville
TENN
ALA
Birmingham
MISS
New Orleans
LA
ARK
Little Rock
MO
ILL
IND
South Bend
MICH
Chicago
Milwaukee
WIS
Duluth
MINN
IOWA
Des Moines
Omaha
NEB
Kansas City
KANS
OKLA
Oklahoma City
TEXAS
Houston
San Antonio
El Paso
N DAK
S DAK
Sioux Falls
MONT
Great Falls
Billings
Butte
WYO
Cheyenne
COLO
Denver
NEW MEX
Albuquerque
ARIZ
Phoenix
Flagstaff
UTAH
Salt Lake City
IDAHO
Boise
NEV
Reno
Las Vegas
CALIF
Los Angeles
San Francisco
Sacramento
Redding
ORE
Medford
Eugene
Portland
WASH
Seattle
Spokane